Everyone on that stretch of Cornish coast, from the lords and ladies and the big and little farmers, to the labourers in the fields and the fishermen along the coast, thought it was almost a duty (if you will forgive the expression!) to support the smugglers who brought in their tea or tobacco or brandy – otherwise how would they be able to afford these pleasures when Parliament put such monstrous taxes on them?

Parson Lanyon himself was of the same opinion, and so was Squire Pellew; so his son, young Dick Pellew, had rubbed shoulders with smugglers all his fifteen years, and admired them too, especially Zach Jewel, and in those happy days when the 'free traders' were able to outwit the excise on every run, nothing ever came near harming them.

Then, like an evil fog, bad times came to the smugglers. The forces of the law became stronger and more persistent under a new leader, and more than once Zach the invincible was in dire need of Dick's help – but who could say whether Zach's luck had run out by itself, or whether something darker and more sinister was happening, and all to do with Roger Kappen, the mysterious stranger who was so full of eager curiosity, and so eager to assure Dick he was his 'friend'. And why was the dumb boy Neil so terrified of Kappen, and what caused the appalling shipwrecks that were happening on their coasts?

This is a story that will thrill anyone who likes tales of adventure and mystery, and will fascinate those who want to know how smugglers actually organized their runs, and the tricks and disguises they used to deliver their goods under the very noses of the excise.

Ruth Manning-Sanders

THE SMUGGLERS

Illustrated by William Stobbs

PUFFIN BOOKS

Puffin Books, Penguin Books Ltd, Harmondsworth, Middlesex, England
Penguin Books, 625 Madison Avenue, New York, New York 10022, U.S.A.
Penguin Books Australia Ltd, Ringwood, Victoria, Australia
Penguin Books Canada Ltd, 2801 John Street, Markham, Ontario, Canada L3R 1B4
Penguin Books (N.Z.) Ltd, 182–190 Wairau Road, Auckland 10, New Zealand

—

First published by Oxford University Press 1962
Published in Puffin Books 1978

—

—

Made and printed in Great Britain
by Richard Clay (The Chaucer Press), Ltd
Bungay, Suffolk
Set in Linotype Baskerville

Contents

I

The Mayfly *Sails for Roscoff*

'Hey! Hey! What's this?'

The voice, scarce above a whisper, but deep-pitched and resonant, spoke out of the quiet night, and from down among the innocent-seeming pile of crab pots in the stern of the *Mayfly*, where I thought to have safely hidden myself, a strong hand grasped my arm and pulled me to my feet. Yes, I had chosen to overlook the fact that Zach's eyes could see in the dark.

'I'm coming with you, Zach!'

'Squire say yes to that?'

'You know very well I haven't asked him.'

'Then you knows very well what *I* do say. You git!'

'But, Zach –'

'Now see here, boy, we've had this out afore.'

I stood irresolute for a moment, listening to the quiet mutter of the tide against the rocks in Jewel's Cove, and the stealthy footfalls of Zach's brothers on the slippery quay. Lucky dogs! *They* were off to Roscoff again, and I, as usual, was to be left out of all the thrilling adventure. Such a night for a run! Star reflections swung and glimmered in the dark water; the steep black cliffs, rising above the Cove on three sides, shut us away from all the world. I drew a deep indignant breath, that brought the smell of brine and tar and tobacco smoke smartly into my nostrils. Hang it all, I *would* go with them!

But Zach's strong hands were already bundling me unceremoniously over the gunwale, and I heard his gurgling laugh as I wet my feet, before landing in a sprawl on the mushy weed among the jetty stones. I got up, shivering with rage and disappointment, and watched the dusky shapes of Job and Matthy and Harry Jewel handing in the gear and unknotting the mooring-line. Now they were all in the boat, now Zach had an oar over the bow and the boat was gliding away from me; now they had the boat turned and the oars out and were rowing strongly, and Zach's voice came floating to me across the ever-widening gap of water.

'So long, boy! See you Monday, all being well.'

And then no sound but the quiet dip and splash of the oars, and the mutter of the tide at my feet.

My eyes, straining against the darkness, watched them making for the deep water, saw the boat lean over before the wind as the shadowy sail went up, and filled, and bore them away round the cliffs, and out of my sight. Then I turned and began to climb the cliffs on my way back home – as reluctant and disappointed a lad as ever breathed.

When I got home, most of the household was long a-bed; but my father, Squire Pellew, was in the summer parlour, hob-nobbing over a bottle of smuggled brandy with his crony, Parson Lanyon. My father had an interest in most of Zach's ventures, though he would never admit it, entrusting the management of all such illicit transactions to Nathaniel Quick, our steward. Of such transactions my father kept up a game of affected ignorance, with himself, and with me, and with everyone – a game which deceived none of us. Though, after a genial glass or two, I once heard him remark, in his dry way, that the smuggler – considered *quite* impersonally – was an honest thief and a public benefactor; and that if the hard-working population of Cornwall paid any heed to the whims of the Parliament men and their monstrous taxes, they would not be able to afford a dish of tea, or a fill of tobacco, or a noggin of brandy from one year's end to the other.

And Parson Lanyon was of the same opinion. So were we all, high and low, from Lord and Lady Trembath, and the big farmers and the little farmers, to the labourers in the fields, the tinners in the mines, and the fishermen along the coast. Indeed, the fishermen, between intervals of laying crab pots and seining for pilchards, made their own runs on dark nights and in calm weather, over to Roscoff and Quimper and back again.

But of all the many dare-devil 'free-traders' up and down the coast, it was Zach Jewel who was my particular friend. He was more than my friend, he was my hero. I thought him the bravest, cleverest, cleanest-living, fairest-dealing fellow that ever walked God's earth; and at that time, when I was in my fifteenth year, I seemed to live for the night when I should slip away with him and his brothers on one of their smuggling ventures. But my father, though tender enough towards the Jewels and all their ways, and though giving me my head in most other matters, was for some, to me, unaccountable reason opposed to my going. I felt it very hard.

2

The Marooning of Roger Kappen

On Monday morning, from dreaming that I was engaged in a brisk fight with a company of riding-officers, I woke to the memory that this was the probable day of Zach's return. Not till night, of course – and what should I do till night? The sun was not yet up, and no one was stirring; but I jumped out of bed, for I was too excited at the thought of night to sleep again. Having flung on my clothes, I ran down to the buttery, and helped myself to a mug of home-brewed ale, a hunk of bread, and a slab of cold pork. I took my lancing-knife, my tin pannikin, and my coil of shore-line and hooks, and started off down through the valley to Garrick Sands.

Not feeling at all like lessons, I was going to take a self-bestowed holiday; for I was at that time a wilful lad, and I went to lessons with Parson Lanyon, or stayed away, much as the whim took me. And I don't think old Lanyon minded which I did; nor yet, I believe, did my father, who, as I have said, let me do in most matters exactly as I pleased. Very like he had some theory of his own about the value of independence in my upbringing. But your thoroughbred Cornishman is difficult to understand, and what went on in my father's intricate mind was not always easy for me to fathom.

As for my mother, who might, had she lived, have exercised a more understandable control over me – she had taken to her bed with an inflammation and died after the night of the great January gale, when we were all, men, women, and children, down on Garrick Sands wrecking, after the coming ashore of the Spanish trader, the *Gracia a Dios,* when I was six years old. I still had a box full of gold pieces of eight and silver *reals* that she and I had picked up from the sands that night. But my mother was to me now only a vague haunting, as of something laughing and lovely, that moved sometimes at the back of my mind when it was not busy about immediate concerns.

My immediate concern on this Monday morning in May was to dig for bait and set my shore-lines before the tide came up over the sands. But I was fated not to set my shore-lines, as you will presently hear. For that was the day when I first set eyes on the man who called himself Roger Kappen.

It was a still morning, with no breath of wind stirring. But the birds were already awake, and in the silence of all else their voices were startlingly clear: the grey-birds shouting at one another from the tops of the tattered elms, the blackbirds whistling, and the wrens singing remarkably sweet and loud from among the tangle of blackthorn and withies on either side of the winding track.

It was a deep, narrow place, this valley, and the rising ground that closed it on either side was strewn with granite boulders and overgrown with furze and bracken. By the time I had neared the end of it the sun was rising and glittering dimly through the elms, though the stream that kept company with the track on my left side was still in shadow, except for an occasional shifting gleam. It was slipping along in a stealthy kind of way, with now and then a chuckle to itself, as if at some private joke. Everything was drenched in dew, and my feet lifted a strong scent of wild peppermint and the stench of rotted flag leaves into the still air. Except for the birds, the whole feeling of the morning was like the holding of a breath: a secret kind of morning.

I surprised a vole that was sitting on the stream-bank, cleaning his whiskers; and he plopped into the water and scurried away downstream. I threw a stone after him; not that I meant him any harm, or could have harmed him had I wished, for he was much too quick for me, but from sheer exhilaration of spirits. Farther on, I came across an adder, coiled up on a granite stone, and I remember wondering idly whether its being abroad so early was a sign of ill luck or good luck. I swung my pannikin at it, and it reared up and hissed and then darted off into the undergrowth. And so, a little foolishly elated at my gesture of defiance, I jumped the stream where it crossed the track, and came out on to the sands.

The tide was still ebbing, and a white fog lay over the sea, so thick that only a thin shimmering edge of water, where it met the sand, was visible, and this was rising and falling with a lazy kind of whisper. It was all so still that where the rocks stood up dark on the sand you could hear the tiny *seep-seep-seep* of the wet barnacles that crusted them. I left my coil of lines on one of these rocks, and went down from the drying sand to the wet. And there, bent double, I began slashing all ways at the sand with my thin, curved knife. The wet sand quivered in front of the knife, and up came the little silvery eels that we call lances. And as they came up I caught them and dropped them into my pannikin.

One had to be mighty quick and mighty deft to catch the slippery little things; and I was so engrossed that when I heard the sound of oars out there in the fog for a second or two I took no notice. And then, of a sudden, I had snatched up my pannikin and was running like a hare to the rock where I had left my lines. And behind that rock I laid me flat, listening now with all my ears.

The sound was coming nearer. I could hear the spatter of the oar blades and the swash of water about the bow of the boat. What boat could it be, coming in on that lonely shore at that hour in the morning? Not the *Mayfly* – not even in fog would Zach risk a daylight landing, and never had I known him to beach on the open sands. My mind raced. A Revenue boat? Could a Revenue cutter be on the prowl for Zach? Could it be sending in a boatload of armed men, to secrete themselves somewhere? Did they hope to take Zach by surprise? Not if I knew it! I blessed my lucky stars that I was there, to watch their every movement, to give the alarm in time, and so save Zach from the inconvenience of a tussle with them.

Very cautiously, and still flat on my stomach, I poked my head round the jutting base of the rock. The sun was well risen now, and the sands were sparkling, though the white fog still lay over the sea. By this time the boat was close in shore, some twenty yards to the west of me. The bow came suddenly clear of the fog, and I saw a man with his hand on the gunwale and one leg over, as if ready to jump. He was wearing a red cap with a tassel and a ragged striped shirt; he was looking past me, up the sands, and his face, with the sun striking on it, seemed almost as thick with grizzled hair as a badger's. All this I saw in the one second before I drew back my head, afraid lest he spy me.

Then I heard the keel strike bottom, and a loud splashing, as it might be of a dozen men leaping into the shallows. And after that there came a din that set all the gulls within earshot wheeling and screaming: hoarse shouts and roaring gusts of laughter, the dull, continuous thump of something heavy against the boat's sides, the rattle of chains, and through it all a kind of gasping and groaning that I ill liked the sound of. No, whoever they were, they were not Revenue men!

Who then? A boatload of drunken pirates? The pirates were very active round our coast and up the Bristol Channel; and a scurvy lot they were, attacking honest smugglers and honest trading vessels with equal indifference. They seldom made a landing, being mostly content with what they could pick up at sea. But when they had had their fill of drink there was no knowing what they would be at. I poked my head round the rock again. All sorts of ominous imaginings were jostling through my mind. I know I was picturing our house going up in flames, and the parsonage a burnt-out shell, and I was wondering what best to do (whether to stay where I was and watch, or make a dash for it up the sands and raise the alarm) when a breeze of wind stirred from the sea, and the fog shuddered and momentarily parted. Then I saw two things simultaneously: out in deep water a two-

masted brig, and inshore the rowing-boat, grounded and partly heeled over, and half a score of ragged men stooping to lift some heavy weight from the bottom of her.

The fog closed down again over the sea before I had time to notice more of the brig than that she was lying to and flying no flag; but the men were moving up the sands

now, and I could see what it was they were carrying: and that was as big a man as I think I had ever set eyes on. His hands were bound behind his back with a lashing of rope, his legs were in irons, and he had a rag of a handkerchief tied tightly over his mouth. The struggle that he made to free himself, heaving his body from side to side and jerking up his knees, was pitiful to see; and the gasping and groaning and muffled cries that came from him were frightful to hear. And the jeering and laughter that came from the ruffians who had hold of him roused such anger in me that I started up from my hiding-place with some wild idea of rushing to his rescue. But when I saw the gleam of the cutlasses the men wore, and, moreover, caught a sight of the ugly pistols that bulged out of the pockets of their ragged coats, I bobbed me down again quicker than I had bounced up, with my heart racing and my mouth gone dry. For I own I was scared nigh out of my wits.

What to do I couldn't tell. Stay where I was and perhaps see murder done? Or shout and show myself and get a bullet through my head for my pains, and, even so, prevent nothing? I shut my eyes and prayed; and then it came to me that it was not likely the wretches would bring a man ashore to murder him, when they could with less trouble have dispatched him out at sea. That thought quietened me, and I opened my eyes and peered once more round the rock, to see what next they would be at.

They were laying him down on the sand. They were knocking the irons off his legs. The moment the irons were off he struggled to his feet; but, his arms being still bound, he lost his balance and fell down again. They let him lie and began running back to the boat; but he was up again and struggling after them, with his head down like a charging bull, and biting at the cord that bound his arms. He fell again, and was up again; and now his arms were free. The men were in a desperate hurry, as if they feared him; one shouted out to him in a foreign tongue – threatening him to keep back, I thought; they were all shouting as they heaved at the boat to get her off the bottom. But before they could float her he had his hand on the bow and was for getting aboard. Then one raised an oar and brought it down on his head with such a thud that had it not been for the moleskin cap he was wearing I think it must have brained him. As it was he staggered, fell, rose again, and began reeling this way and that – into the water and out on to the sand, and then a few paces up the sand, and round and round as if he had no notion where he was, or which way he was walking. But he turned at last and was for following them again, when a shot rang out, and a bullet went zipping past him, to bury itself with a fine sputter in the sand some yards behind him. He flung himself down and rolled over on his face. More shots followed, but they went wide; for either the men were so drunk that they could not aim straight or they did not mean to hit him. They were afloat now; and the last I saw of that boat was her rudder leaping clean from the water with the frenzy of their rowing. And then she disappeared into the fog.

3
I Rescue a Strange Character

I jumped to my feet and raced to the prostrate man.

'Are you *very* badly hurt?' I panted.

He turned over at the sound of my voice, and his eyes stared at me; a peculiar light blue colour they were, very bright and cold-looking. Blood was oozing from under his cap and over the rag that gagged his mouth. He raised himself a little and put one great hand feebly to the tight knot at the back of his head; but I cut the knot with my lancing-knife and snatched the rag from his mouth. He gave a sickly grin.

'Hurt, mate?' he said. 'Yes, I *be* hurt – bad. But not to death.'

'Stay where you are a moment, then,' said I, though I am sure he was in no state to move. And I ran to my rock, tipped the eels out of my pannikin, and raced over the sands to the stream for water.

When I got back he was sitting up, weakly trying to pull the cap from his head; but it was all matted up with the blood. I put the pannikin to his lips, and he drank eagerly; and then, with what remained of the water, I busied myself about his head. But I had to run to the stream twice more before I got the cap unstuck. I'm afraid it was roughly done, and he groaned once or twice.

'Easy on, mate,' he said, 'or you'll have off head and all.'

I apologized and fell to my work once more, and had the cap off at last, when to my surprise, for he did not look old, I found that his head was as bald as an egg. Altogether, now that I had time to notice what he was like, I saw that he was a peculiar-looking man. His face was all one colour – a kind of pale yellow – and smooth and hairless, and he had very high cheek-bones, and a great mouth on him full of big, strong teeth. Everything about him was big and strong, his hands especially so; and the backs of those hands were covered with yellow freckles, and, oddly, with a growth of golden hair.

I got my shirt off and tore it in strips and bandaged the wound on the side of his head; and he sat squinting up at me out of one china-blue eye, the other being covered with the bandage.

'What's your name?' I asked.

'Name?' he said hesitatingly, almost as if he had forgotten it. 'Name, is it? Well now – Roger's my name. Roger Kappen.'

'Kappen?' I repeated. 'How d'you spell it?'

'I don't spell it,' said he. 'Never have. So you can spell it any way you like.'

'Well,' I said, 'it's a new name to me. You'll not be from these parts?'

'No,' said he. 'Not from these parts – exactly.'

'Where then?'

He was silent for a moment. Then he said, 'Now see here, mate. You mean well by me, I'll own. But I'm like a thing lost me latitude. So don't you go plaguing me with no more questions till I've found me bearings.'

'No, of course not,' I said. 'I'm sorry.'

And I told him my own name – Dick Pellew.

'Dick!' he repeated. 'That's a good name. I had a brother once by name of Dick. But he went round land [he meant died], sonny, five years back, and left me stranded.'

I almost asked him in what way stranded, but remembered in time that I was not to plague him.

'And seeing as here I be,' he went on, 'stranded once more, as you might say, what do you mean to do with me, Dick?'

I hadn't given the matter a thought, but I answered promptly, 'Take you home, of course.'

'And where might home be?'

I told him.

'But it's a goodish step,' I said. 'Do you think you can walk? Or shall I get help?'

'I'll make shift to walk,' said he. 'But give us a heave up, Dick.'

I held out my hand to him, and he took it in a grip that made me wince. And there he stood on his feet, swaying. Then he put an arm over my shoulder, and the weight of him soon had me sweating. And so, with frequent staggerings and pausings (these last as much for my sake as his), we zigzagged like a couple of drunkards up over the sands and began to crash our way through the valley.

'I'll sit down and rest me here a bit,' said he, when we came to the stone where I had seen the adder.

I was right glad to rest myself, and I sat at his feet on a clump of rushes. He looked up at the sky and across at the stream and the catkinned willows. 'It's a lonesome spot, this here is, Dick,' he remarked.

'I suppose it is,' I said. 'I hadn't thought about it.'

'And your father, this here Squire Pellew, he owns it all, as you might say?'

'More or less, I suppose,' I answered vaguely. 'But we're not rich folk.'

'No,' he repeated, 'not rich folk.'

And then we got up, and staggered on.

It must have been close on noon before we reached the head of the valley, where a bridle path ran east and west, and the old church reared its grey tower between the Pure Drop Inn and the parsonage; and a few labourers' cottages fronted a flat green where geese were grazing. Pellew Manor stood farther back, uphill among trees. And, a mile or two farther north, ran the turnpike road – the only road there was in our end of the county.

By the time we got to the Pure Drop, Kappen seemed nigh to fainting; and as to myself, I ached in every limb from the weight of him. So I pushed him down on a bench by the door, and went in and fetched him a dram of brandy. And who should come trotting along the bridle path at that moment but Parson Lanyon, mounted on his dapple-grey mare, and looking very spruce, with his powdered bag-wig shining white under his tricorne hat, and his chubby rosy face, with the large bulbous grey eyes beaming at me from behind his horn glasses. 'The cherub in spectacles' my father called him; and indeed he was round enough and plump enough for the fattest cherub of them all – though he could be a petulant cherub at times.

'Ah, Dick!' says he, trotting over to the inn door and

pulling the mare up sharply. 'So we both forgot it was Monday! It won't do, sir, it won't do! "Six days shalt thou labour" – but what have we here?'

I was beginning to tell him, but at that moment Kappen reeled on the bench and fell flat in some kind of faint.

Parson Lanyon slid off the mare, flung the reins over her neck, and began to fuss and shout. 'Here, Dan, here I say! Here, Bart – here, Jim – devil take you all! Is this a Christian country? Here's a man dying at your door and not a soul heeding!'

Out ran Dan Hooper, the landlord, and out ran Bart Thomas, the barman, with the cloth in his hand with which he had been wiping the beer mugs, and out ran Jimmy Bandy, the parson's stable boy.

'Aye,' said Dan, staring at the figure tumbled sideways on the bench, 'he looks wisht, sure enough. And what'll we do with him now, sir?'

'*Do*, you numbskull!' exclaimed Parson Lanyon. 'Take him by the shoulders and the feet, and carry him into the parsonage. And do you, Dick, get on the mare, and ride like the devil for Doctor Treglown – and don't you come back without him, if you have to scour the country!'

Dan stepped up to the bench and reluctantly took Kappen by the shoulders. 'I doubt we'd drop him, sir,' said he. 'The man's that heavy.'

'Pooh!' said Parson Lanyon. 'I'll give you a hand.'

I vaulted into the mare's saddle and galloped off. And, glancing back, I saw the four of them staggering away under their load towards the parsonage gate, with Parson Lanyon's hat tumbled off on the grass and his wig all awry on his head.

4
Jewel's Place

'Pellew,' said Parson Lanyon, bursting into the parlour just as my father and I were finishing dinner, 'Doctor Treglown's an ass!'

'I don't agree,' said my father. 'Take a seat. Have some port. Excellent stuff! We mayn't get much more of this particular brand, so Nathaniel tells me ... And by the way,' he went on, as he filled the parson's glass, 'have you heard the rumour of a new Excise officer coming to Priddy-mouth? What is it they say about new brooms?'

'Pooh!' said Parson Lanyon. 'New brooms can be accommodated.'

'Not all of them,' said my father. 'You forget, parson, there is such a thing as devotion to duty . . . Yes, devotion to duty,' he repeated, thoughtfully contemplating his fingernails. 'I admire it myself.'

'So do we all admire it – in moderation,' said Parson Lanyon. 'But if not accommodated – then diddled, sir! Here's to the Jewels and all honest free-traders!' He raised his glass, then he put it down again. 'But Dick must drink this toast, too,' said he. 'Come now, Pellew, don't be stingy with the lad!'

My father poured me out half a glassful, and we all drank: Parson Lanyon and myself loudly repeating the toast to the 'honest free-traders', my father quirking up his eyebrows, but saying nothing.

'Now then,' said the parson, holding out his glass to be refilled, 'what did I come here to tell you? Oh yes, that Treglown's an ass! After he came down from seeing to that poor fellow – what's his name – Kappen, he had the impudence to tell me that the man was shammocking. "Shammocking!" I exclaimed. "Haven't you eyes? Didn't you look at his head?"

'"Oh yes, I looked at his head," says he, "and put a stitch or two in it. And I'll not deny he's been roughly handled. But he put a faint on for your benefit all the same."

'"Why should he do that?" says I.

'"I can't tell you," says he. "Unless for the convenience of keeping his own counsel. Who is he? Where does he come from? What's the reason for his being treated as he was? I couldn't get a word out of him. In my opinion he's a shifty customer – and an ugly one."

'"It has pleased the Lord our God to make some of us beautiful to look upon and some of us ugly," says I. "And if you doubt it, take a glance in the mirror when you get home." Not very Christian of me this, I'll own, but I was nettled. "And as to not getting a word out of him," says I, "it doesn't surprise me, if that's the way you regard him!"

'So he laughed and left me. I sent Kappen up a dish of broth; and after giving him time to settle down a bit, I went upstairs myself, and talked to him soothingly, and he told me his story without my even asking for it. So much for that fool Treglown!'

'And what was his story?' asked my father.

'I'm coming to that,' said the parson. 'It seems this Kappen was one of the crew of a licensed privateer, sailing under letters of marque, all fair and square and above board. And if they did a little free-trading on their own account – who's blaming them for that? But when it came to attacking our own trading ships, like any scoundrelly pack of pirates, "Then," says Kappen, "I didn't see eye to eye with them, sir. More especially as they didn't stop at theft, but went on to murder." So he up like a man and spoke his mind. And what did his blackguardly shipmates do but set on him – thirty-six to one – and clap him in irons, and put him ashore, not caring whether he lived or died. And a mercy it was Dick found him! Well, that's the story, and *I* say the man's a hero!'

Parson Lanyon had worked himself up into a fever of enthusiasm over his strange guest; and, for my part, I was glad to know that I had rescued a hero. But my father stroked his chin in a thoughtful kind of way. I think he had more faith in Doctor Treglown's judgement than in the parson's.

'Of course,' he said, 'the man must be seen to.'

'Seen to!' exclaimed Parson Lanyon. 'I mean to set him up, sir, set him up!'

'Set him up?' said my father. 'In what way?'

'In any honest way he chooses,' answered the parson. 'He can work for me, if he likes. And you've an empty cottage, haven't you?'

My father gave a flicker of a smile. 'Well, as to that – we must wait and see.'

I left them talking and wandered out to saddle my cob, Diamond, and rode off to visit Gracie Winkey, the old dame who lived in a tumbledown barn of a house on the cliffs above Jewel's Cove. She was called Winkey because she kept a 'kiddleywink' – one of those houses of entertainment so called because you could get as much liquor as you wished at any time by winking at the kettle; though there was no need to do any winking in Gracie's case. Nobody would have dared to question what that old woman did: she was reputed to be a witch, and traded on her reputation.

When I went into her kitchen, I found her at work on a small wax figure, into which she was sticking pins with great relish. The figure was wearing the semblance of a riding-officer's hat.

'Who's that?' I asked.

'Who be that?' says she. 'Stinking great Tidecombe, that be! Blast him! May his eyeballs drop from their sockets, and his sword arm wither to his side!' She rammed two pins into the figure's face and three more into his right arm. 'May he come a crack among the moorstones this night, and break the two great legs of him!' (Six pins went into each leg now.) 'I aren't taking no chances. We'll have our dear boys home safe this night.'

'Tidings of them?' I asked eagerly. For sometimes a returning fisherman might bring news of having caught sight of the *Mayfly*, hovering outside the three-mile limit, and waiting on night.

'Tidings!' echoed Gracie. 'Where's your Scripture? "A bird of the air shall carry the voice." There come a crow to my window – that's all the tidings I do need.'

All this while her little knobbly hands were busy with the pins, till the wax figure fairly bristled with them.

'Now see,' says she, and carried the figure over to the hearth and set it down among the ashes. 'Iss, iss,' says she, glancing at the clock. 'I'll give 'ee till it strikes to shed your tears. Here they come! See 'em a-trickling over his jawbone!'

The figure began to drip; the wax flowed over the pin-heads and dropped among the ashes. The pins themselves fell out, one after the other. In a few moments the clock struck five, and there was nothing left of 'stinking great Tidecombe' but a little pool of bubbling wax, matted with tarnished pins.

Gracie gave a cackle of laughter, picked up the fire shovel, and tossed the wax under a faggot. Her eyes, that were the colour of the sea in deep places, shone with a kind of good-humoured malice.

'Now, my handsome,' said she. 'What can I do for 'ee?'

'Oh, nothing,' said I. 'I just came for a chat.'

I told her of my morning's adventure, and she sniffed and snorted, and said she hoped good might come of it. And then I left her (for I was that impatient for night that I couldn't stay still) and went on to Jewel's Place.

The Kiddleywink and Jewel's Place were the only two houses on the cliffs above Jewel's Cove. Jewel's Place was a barren-looking granite building, standing four square, with a highish wall of great thickness shutting in the yard that enclosed it. The yard was littered with all the innocent gear of a fisherman's trade – crab pots, nets, oars, sails, cork floats, and piles of wreckwood. But, tucked under the wall, close to the iron gates on the seaward side, were three little brass cannons, which did not look so innocent. At the back of the yard was a well, and beside the well, covered with a granite slab, and hidden under a pile of crab pots, was the entrance to a tunnel.

The geography of this tunnel was as familiar to me as the palm of my hand. One branch of it led down to the caves that riddled the cliffs at the back of the Cove. Another branch ran for a great distance inland, and came up into a dense thicket of furze bushes behind Pellew Manor. It was to this thicket, on the night of a landing, that the loading gang sometimes brought their donkeys, well greased from head to tail, and with their hoofs muffled in old stockings. On such nights my father would make a point of going to bed betimes, of snoring extra loud, and of coming down in the morning with the bland remark that he had never slept better in his life.

I found old Zebedee, the Jewels' father, sawing up wreckwood in the yard, with his wife holding the ends of the planks for him. They were such a little couple, she bright and sharp like a small bird, he gnarled and wizened like a hobgoblin, that one wondered how they managed to produce between them four such strapping sons as Zach and Job and Matthy and Harry.

'Atternoon, boy Dick,' says Zeb.

'Atternoon, my lover,' says Sarah, his wife. 'Had your dinner, have 'ee?'

'Why yes,' I said, 'some two hours agone. And we drank to all your healths.'

'What, drink to we?' says Sarah. 'Squire and all?'

'Yes, my father, too,' said I.

'That's all right, then,' said Sarah, mighty pleased. 'Hear that, did 'ee, Zeb?'

' 'Course I heared,' says Zeb. He chuckled. 'Us had visitors last night, Dick. Tidecombe and his gang. Aye, they'd been down to Cove and found naught, and they come up here – and found naught, though they rummaged all ways. See that shed door swinging wide? She were locked up fast and tidy when they come. "I'll trouble you for the key of that shed," says Tidecombe.

' "No trouble at all," says I, "for I ain't got it. My son Zach belongs to keep the key of that place in his pocket."

' "And where be he?" says Tidecombe.

' "Where he should be," says I, "away to sea with his nets."

' "I must see what's in the shed," says Tidecombe.

' "You'll be none the better off when you have seen," says I.

' "That's not my opinion," says he.

'So he gets one of his gang to break the lock with the claw-hammer. Then he swings open the door and in he marches, and finds naught but me old cart and donkey harness, and a few bits of tools put by from the time I worked to bal; and out he comes looking down his nose, and they all get on their hosses and ride off, the men laughing, and him sweering on 'em. But the odd part of it is,' Zeb screwed up one of his little goblin eyes in a tremendous wink, 'me not being able to lock up the shed again, all the gear what was in it took itself off in the night. You step over and have a look.'

I stepped over and looked in. 'Why yes, there's nothing in the shed at all!' said I.

'And how come that, do you think?' said Zeb, with another tremendous wink. 'I set the value of that there gear at five pund, five shellin'. And if 'tis stole, who's to blame? Why that Tidecombe, to be sure! I'll larn him to come breaking open doors, so's a man cain't keep his property safe from thieving hands! I'll put him to court! The law'll be on my side – see if it wain't!'

I laughed. I knew it would be. Trust any local magistrate to jump at a chance of putting a riding-officer in the wrong! Yes, Zeb would get his five pounds, five shillings all right! And, as it turned out, he did; with another pound added for a new lock and 'repairs to the door'. And, with the new lock, the donkey cart and harness and the few bits of tools mysteriously came back into the shed. Zeb said the thief must have repented and returned them, and there would be joy in heaven over that caper. But all this was some weeks on from the Monday in May I am telling of.

It seemed to me that the sun would never go down that day; but it set at last, and twilight came, and then dark. And with night came a troop of men, farm labourers, and tinners, with Zeb Jewel leading, slithering silently and cautiously down the steep path from the top of the cliffs. We all gathered on the small quay. The breeze stirred in our ears, and the little dark waves gurgled at our feet. And we talked in whispers.

'See a light, can 'ee?'

'No.'

'Iss!'

'No!'

'Iss – see that?'

'No, boy, that bain't no light. 'Tis yon gait star peeking at itself in the flood. Naught else.'

'But see yon! Over to west'ard!'

'Iss, iss! '*Tis* a light, sure 'nough!'

'That'll be them, boys! Show 'em a glim, Andy!'

'You boys sartin all's clear in shore?'

'Aye. Tidecombe's galloping off to Hey's Mouth after a red herrin'.'

Thus assured, Andy took a lantern from under his coat, and waved it in a circle, three times. Then he pushed it back under his coat with a stifled exclamation. 'There be someone coming!'

'Well, what d'you think? 'Tis only parson. He never could get down without loosing a stone or two. Too much in a hurry, he be.'

And, sure enough, in a minute or two, there was Parson Lanyon, with his head tied up in a turban, stockings drawn over his boots, and a pistol stuck into either pocket of his long coat – looking much like a plump little make-believe pirate, as he came puffing and panting along the quay towards us.

'Bless us all!' he muttered. 'I nearly broke my neck! I saw their light from the cliff-top. Hand over that lantern, Andy.'

Andy handed over the lantern, and it disappeared under the parson's coat-tails.

The light out to sea had vanished, but there was the *Mayfly*'s sail now, a blur against the brightening stars.

'There's too many of these old stars,' someone said querulously. 'Tain't no fitty night, at all!'

And then the sail went down, and we saw the dim hull drawing nearer and nearer, and heard the stealthy dip of oars and their faint creaking against the wooden thole-pins.

And so the *Mayfly* came in, lying deep in the water with her load, and towing a goodly procession of tubs, roped together, behind her.

Not one word said Zach as he leaped ashore; not one word said anybody. All hands were now working with demonic energy at the unloading; while Parson Lanyon

moved in the thick of the crowd, showing the lantern now here, now there, where it was most needed. I could hear his heavy breathing, as he puffed from this man to that, and every now and then the happy little chuckles that came from him. And I knew he was enjoying himself like any naughty boy.

'Where be the mokes?' asked Zach, when all was landed.

'Back of our place,' said Zeb.

'Then us don't need use the tunnel,' said Zach. ' 'Tis up the cliff, boys.'

And off we all set, dragging and carrying our loads – sacks of tobacco, and oilskin bags of tea, and barrels of brandy and rum and gin – with Parson Lanyon scrambling in the rear, carrying the blown-out lantern.

5
An Anker of Brandy

At the top of the cliff, behind Jewel's Place, the well-greased and stocking-hoofed train of donkeys stood nibbling at the short furze; and old Gracie Winkey, all but invisible, except where the glim from her clay pipe wavered across the deep wrinkles on her cheeks, sat on a boulder, watching lest the animals stray, and awaiting her share of the spoils. Everyone treated her with the greatest respect; for though the men knew she was on their side, they knew, also, that a chance word might offend her, and then let the unlucky speaker of that word look out for cramps in the night, or his cow gone dry, or the rot breaking out among his little flock of sheep.

For her share of the night's haul – an anker of brandy, a bag of tea, and a small sack of tobacco – Gracie was expected to pay but a few shillings; and if she didn't choose to pay, not even Zach Jewel himself would have the effrontery to demand it of her. I think of all that crowd only the parson and myself had any doubts of her supernatural powers; and even we liked to keep on the right side of her. Because you never knew.

So, while Sexton Andy carried Gracie's spoils across to the Kiddleywink for her, the rest of us silently busied ourselves about the loading of the donkeys: two casks, or two sacks, or four bags to an animal, slung across the back by a single girth and nicely balanced on either side.

We were about to set off across the moor, and Parson Lanyon had already bidden us good night and puffed his way homeward on foot (since it was too dark to ride), when we heard a low whistle in the darkness ahead, and a small man, Ellick the shoemaker (nicknamed 'Tiger' in derision of his feeble physique), came running full tilt towards us.

'Tidecombe's on the rampage, and he's coming this way!' stuttered Tiger, as soon as he could catch his breath.

'How so?' says one. 'There was lights flashed for un down to Hey's Mouth, and us seed him set off yonder.'

'Aye, but he's been gone and come back again! He passed my place at a gallop, sweering on his men. There's no going that road. And there's no staying here! He'll be on you afore you can get all that gear back through the tunnel to the caves – and what about them mokes to give 'ee away?'

'Let un come!' said Gracie Winkey. 'Wheer's your spunk? You've got guns a-plenty, ain't you?'

'Nay,' says Zach. 'Shoot when us has to, not afore.'

To use arms against an Excise officer was to risk hanging – as, indeed, was the very carrying of arms by a smuggler, whether he used them or not. Everybody knew it. But everybody knew, too, that no jury in the country would bring in a verdict of guilty if they could help it.

Zach turned to me. 'Squire a-bed, boy?'

'Sure to be, hours ago,' I said.

'Then 'tis down through the Gurgoes to the pond,' said Zach.

So, instead of taking our way across the moor at the back of Jewel's Place to Trevy Downs, where, among the tinworkings, the smugglers had a large hide-out under a tinners' hut, we turned to the right and plunged down into the Gurgoes. This was a narrow depression between two hilly bits of country, and so grown over with furze and brambles that it formed a kind of shallow tunnel. Into this tunnel, then, we led the long-suffering donkeys, feeling our way among the prickly furze, starting the stonechats and pipits that were sleeping there, pushing aside the trailing bramble shoots that barred our way, getting finely scratched on face and hands. Except for a muttered oath when someone stumbled against a furze root, we walked in almost complete silence, and in a muffle of darkness, with not so much as a star piercing the thick growth over our heads.

'Hark!' whispered someone suddenly.

We all stood still to listen. Over the moor, away to our

left, and high above us, came the faint *thud, thud,* of galloping hoofs.

'Tidecombe's gang!'

'But they'll turn back when they meet old Gracie,' someone said. 'Not a man of 'em dares face she, not if Tidecombe takes the whip to 'em.'

The faint thud of hoofs faded away to the south of us. Then, after a while, we heard it again, more to the north.

'What did I tell 'ee? They're running from her!'

'She best have minded her own business, and let 'em pass down to Cove,' muttered Zach. 'There's naught in the boat but the crab pots. Now, who knows where they'll make for? We best way hurry along, boys.'

We started once more on our toilsome way. But it was a full hour before we came out of the Gurgoes and crossed over the stream in a dip behind Pellew House. On the other side of this dip was a marshy meadow, and in the meadow was a small duck pond. The ducks had been penned for the night against foxes, and the pens stood well back from the pond. It was a circular pond, and shallow, not more than two feet deep, and its waters did not splay out into the meadow, but were held in check by a curve of stout timber completely encircling its edge.

It was quite a showpiece, was our duck pond, as those of us who were in the secret knew. I don't suppose there was another like it in the world. For you had but to take up a lever that lay behind the pens, fit it into a deep groove in the timber, give a stout pull, and, hey presto! round swung the pond, gravelly bottom, little fishes and all – and the ducks, if they happened to be swimming on it – and there, gaping open, was a strongly vaulted and capacious cellar, where any amount of smuggled gear could be hidden away.

So, with the donkeys halted and the girths loosened,

the pond swung round, and the cellar open to the night, we swiftly unloaded. And when the cellar was packed, and the tell-tale girths flung down among the barrels, the pond back in position, and the lever stowed away once more behind the pens, the company dispersed in twos and threes, to make their way home by devious ways; most of them leaving their donkeys to make the best of *their* way home by themselves, since a solitary man, or a solitary beast, calls for less remark than the two of them together would.

Tiger Ellick was rewarded with a small tub of brandy for his timely news. And this he insisted on carrying away with him. And since he was a small, frail man, and since I myself felt too excited and wide awake to return to my bed, I volunteered to go along with him, and take turn and turn about with carrying the tub.

All went well with us as long as we kept under the stone hedges of Pellew fields; the cattle blew out their breath in inquisitive snorts as we disturbed them at their grazing, and the sheep got to their feet and scampered off in a huddle as we passed them by. And that was all the company we met. But to reach Carn Crowse, the hamlet where Tiger lived, we had to come out on to a bridle path. It was Tiger's turn to carry the tub, and he was hurrying along at my side, nigh bent double with the weight of it when we heard a horseman approaching at a brisk trot.

On the instant I was off the path and scrambling up a bit of a bank into a growth of bracken. But Tiger stood stockstill, as if the strength had gone from his legs with panic.

'Halt! Who goes there? Stand in the King's name!' came a loud voice and a lantern swung into poor Tiger's face as he sank to the ground beside the brandy tub.

'So ho!' says the rider (one of Tidecombe's men, as I could see by his hat). 'I've caught you, have I? And what are you doing with that tub?'

'I – I – f-found it,' stammered Tiger.

'And where did you find it? Come, come, speak up, man!'

'Down to – down to Hey's Mouth, bu-buried in the sand,' says Tiger. 'I own I done wrong, sir; but – but I'm a poor man, with n-nine childer, and my wife sick in the bed with the doctor. I was looking for a bit of firewood, I was, to – to heat her up a sup of milk, and this here thrust itself under my nose, as you might say, I th-thought as 'twould do her, and me, too, a power of good; but I'll hand it over, sir, if that's your will. But I'm sh-shaking with the f-fever, sir, as you can see; it's – it's the ague t-takes me, sir, now and agin, since the time I was out f-foreign. And if I might make so b-bold, sir, as to b-beg you for one little drink, I could maybe rise to me feet and g-get me home.'

The Excise man looked round him at the dark night. Nothing stirred. He listened. Not a sound save the faint clacker of Tiger's chattering teeth. Then he laughed.

'All right, you rascal,' he said. 'I could do with a drink myself. But no tales, mind!'

'No, n-no tales, your worship,' says Tiger, with a shaking chuckle.

The Excise man felt in his pocket and drew out a large clasp-knife. 'There's a corkscrew in it,' says he. 'Broach away!'

Tiger fumbled with the knife. He fumbled with the corkscrew. By the light of the lantern which the Excise man, leaning from his horse, held down towards him, I could see Tiger's shaking hand as it rattled the corkscrew against the tub.

'Hurry, man, hurry! I can't stop here all night,' says the rider, glancing round him.

'It's – it's the ague, sir; me hands is numb and useless.'

With an impatient exclamation the rider slid from his horse, flung the reins to Tiger, snatched the knife from him, and stooped to broach the tub himself.

The slydom of that Tiger! No sooner were the reins in his hands than the ague left him; he was up in the saddle in a trice and galloping away into the night.

The Excise man flung down the knife with a curse, gave a shout, and started to run up the path after the fast-vanishing horse and rider.

The tub stood lonely on the path. I slid down the bank, hoisted the tub on to my shoulder, and carried it home.

6

'Nicely Stuffed'

'Dick,' says my father, raising his eyebrows when I came down yawning to breakfast, 'I'm afraid, my lad, you were late a-bed last night. As for myself, I retired early, and spent a most peaceful night. Nothing to disturb an honest man's rest – no owls, no badgers, no foxes – at least, I think not?'

'Yes, there were foxes abroad, sir,' said I. 'I was wakeful, and I took a turn as far as the duck pond, to see that all was secure there.'

'And was all secure there, Dick?'

'All was secure,' said I. 'The foxes were barking round about Jewel's Place, but they didn't come down to the pond.'

'I'm glad of that,' said my father. He took a meditative draught of ale. Then he gave a twitch to the flowered gown he always wore of a morning, together with a voluminous turban to cover his close-cropped head, not getting into wig and coat till he went out and about. 'The foxes wouldn't pick up anything at Jewel's Place, I expect?' he went on. 'Because I fancy – I may be wrong, of course – but I *fancy* Jewel doesn't keep ducks?'

'He has no ducks up there at the moment,' I said.

Whereat my father's long lips flickered into a smile.

My father had a whimsical way with him. It was understood between us that he was to hear nothing, and to know nothing – except by innuendo which we both enjoyed – about any night adventure. Even the secret of the duck pond was not admittedly known by him, though he had himself given orders for the pond to be made, with its caulked teak bottom and edging; and he would sometimes show it to visitors. And speaking of the pond brings me to the events of that morning.

I went to my lessons, not that I had any inclination for them, but because I wished for news of Roger Kappen. I found Parson Lanyon in a most uncherubic mood, irritable and yawning. And when I added my yawns to his, he clapped my Horace shut, told me my wits were wool-gathering, and advised me to go home.

I asked him how the invalid was.

'Invalid?' says the parson, instantly recovering his temper. 'Not much invalid about him! I bade him rest quietly in bed, but he said it didn't come natural to him. He's dressed and gone out. Amazing stamina! You may come across him about the place somewhere, though it's my belief he's keeping out of the way of Doctor Treglown. These tough-looking fellows are often surprisingly touchy.

I don't blame him! Would you like it, Dick, if someone regarded you as a shifty and ugly customer?'

'I certainly shouldn't – if I knew,' I said.

'Ah, but these things can be sensed. It's not what we say, Dick, it's what we feel. "As a man thinketh in his heart", remember.'

I didn't want him to get moralizing at me, so I told him of our adventure with the tub and the Excise man. Whereat he laughed heartily, and said he would have the tub carried round to Tiger under his housekeeper's petticoats, when she next rode pillion to market behind Jimmy Bandy. Then he remarked that if my wits were wool-gathering his own were no better, and that he would take a nap.

I drew the curtains across the window for him, and saw him settled down in his armchair. Then I went out into the bright morning, with its scents of sea and thyme and clover.

I didn't see Kappen anywhere about the place; but when I got back to Pellew Manor, there he was, leaning up against one of the park gate-posts. I asked him how he was feeling, and was surprised afresh to notice how big he was, and with such great hands on him as I'd never before seen on any man.

'Well, me head throbs, and me legs is stiff,' said he. 'Otherwise pretty good. You've got company up to your place.'

'Have we?' I said, not greatly interested. There was always someone coming and going.

'Riding-officer,' said Kappen.

'What! Tidecombe?' I was all alert now.

'If that be his name,' said Kappen. 'And a couple of men with him. By the ways – what was that about a duck pond, Dick?'

I stared at him. 'Duck pond?' says I. 'How–?'

'Now all right, son,' said Kappen. 'I happened to hear tell as you had a fine duck pond.'

'Well, we have a duck pond.'

'Would you say now as it's the pride and joy of your father's heart?'

'I believe he is a little proud of it,' I answered, feeling quite at sea, and no little troubled. 'It's well made.'

'Oh, so it's well made, is it?'

'Look here, Kappen,' I burst out, 'what are you getting at?'

'I'm not getting at nothing,' answered Kappen sulkily. ' 'Twere parson's stable lad told me about the duck pond. But I'll be going along now, for the old sun do make me head throb.'

He strode off with his swinging seaman's walk towards the parsonage. I hurried on through the park, where horses and cows were grazing. Pellew House was part manor, part farm, and all a bit unkempt and rough, I suppose, my father having as much as he could do to keep things going. When I got into the parlour I found him fully dressed, sitting under the window with Tidecombe, over a glass of innocent home-brewed. He gave me a quizzical, sidelong glance, and introduced me. And I bowed in my best, formal manner.

'Stinking great Tidecombe', as Gracie Winkey dubbed him, was a red-faced, tight-lipped man, well set-up, with a back straight as a ramrod. It didn't seem that the old woman's pin-sticking had done him much harm as yet.

'You see, sir,' said he, 'I've got my duty to do.'

'Naturally, officer,' answered my father. 'Devotion to duty is an admirable thing. And if I can help you, I am at your disposal. Now what exactly is it you would like to know?'

'Well, sir,' went on Tidecombe, 'it goes without saying that I am far from suspecting you personally as I am from suspecting an unborn babe.' (Oh are you, you sly fox! thought I.) 'But I have received information that a party of men with donkeys carrying contraband were seen in your grounds last night. As I understand it, they were approaching the house. And certainly there were fellows abroad in the early hours of this morning, skulking their way home. I met several, some with donkeys, and some without, and carrying nothing. And so the contraband must have been deposited –'

'Good heavens, officer!' interrupted my father. 'All this going on last night, do you say? And I hearing nothing! It was a singularly peaceful night as far as I was concerned. I must say I never slept better.'

'I have my warrant to make a search, sir,' said Tidecombe stiffly.

'Of course, of course,' agreed my father. 'Duty is duty, as I think you observed. Search the grounds, search the house, search from garret to cellar! You shall have all my keys. Most distressing affair this, for both of us. Ring the bell, Dick.'

I rang, and old Nathaniel, our steward, came in.

'Bring my house keys, Nathaniel,' says my father, 'and the keys of any outbarns that happen to be locked. Bring the cellar-book, also.'

Nathaniel, after a derisive look at officer Tidecombe, said, 'Yes, sir', and went; and returned in a few moments with two bunches of keys and the cellar-book.

My father handed them over to Tidecombe. 'Here you are, officer,' said he. 'The more thoroughly you search, the better pleased I shall be. You won't wish me to accompany you? Very well, Dick and I will remain here and await your return. If you find anything of a suspicious nature –

well, you have the law at your back, and that's all I can say.'

Tidecombe bowed stiffly and went out. My father remarked that it was a hot morning, and dabbed at his forehead with a lace handkerchief. 'Only a wild rumour, I expect, Dick?'

'Of course, it can be nothing but a rumour, sir,' I answered. 'Though I wonder who –'

'Well, never mind about that,' said my father. 'A pleasant fellow, Tidecombe. I think we'll invite him to dine with us. Let me see –' he gave the merest twitch of a smile. 'A brace of ducks, eh, Dick? And after dinner he may be interested to see our duck pond.'

I burst out laughing. But my father merely twinkled, and remarked that this running of contraband was a serious business; and that if I would ring the bell again, he would give an order about the ducks.

Meanwhile Tidecombe and his two men were stamping through the house, unlocking cupboards, flinging open presses, peering behind hangings and under beds, rummaging and poking here, there, and everywhere. Tidecombe was a hot and determined man, and the longer he searched and found nothing, the hotter he became. I wandered out to the foot of the great staircase, and heard him swearing at his men under his breath. Then they all came clattering down and betook themselves to the cellars, Tidecombe with the cellar-book open in his hand. I knew there was nothing in the wine cellar but what was listed in the book, carefully set down in Nathaniel's spiky handwriting, with the amounts and dates of purchase from legitimate wine merchants. Tidecombe was biting his lip with vexation when he came up again, but his men were grinning from ear to ear. They were well aware that peace-offerings in the shape of an anker or two would be waiting for them up under the Standing Stones on the high moor by and by, if all went well with this business. *They* had no desire to catch anyone out.

'Well, did you find anything?' asked my father.

'Nothing so far,' said Tidecombe.

'I'm glad of that,' said my father. 'Would you like Dick to show you the round of the barns and stables?'

'No, I thank you,' answered Tidecombe curtly.

I followed them out all the same. One of the men gave me a wink.

' 'Tis a waste of our time, I'm thinking,' said he.

'I'm thinking the same,' I answered. 'I have an idea your pocket's unbuttoned.'

'Is it so?' says he. 'But my money's safe, I reckon?'

'I have an idea you dropped some in the wine cellar – beside the ale barrel,' said I. For Nathaniel had just whispered to me that there was a trifle of silver there 'for the men's trouble'.

'Maybe I did,' said he. 'I'll take a look presently.'

Tidecombe was now hot on the scent in barns and stables – hotter than he knew. For sunk in the well by the horse trough in the stableyard were the hogsheads of port, waiting to be bottled for daily consumption; and the bins in the stable were but half full of bran and oats, and had false bottoms to them concealing bags of tea. And in the straw-covered pavement under the hoofs of my father's stallion, Wallace (who happened, most opportunely, to be in his stall that morning), there was one paving stone that could be lifted; and down below, the hollow space that extended the whole length of the stable was handy for storing tobacco.

Tidecombe gave up at last and went back to my father to report reluctantly that he had found nothing.

'Then the rascals must have gone on somewhere else,'

said my father, 'after impertinently making free of my grounds for transport. But you'll stay and dine with us, officer? A brace of ducks, nicely stuffed, and with some good apple sauce, wouldn't come amiss?'

Tidecombe agreed that they wouldn't.

'And as luck will have it,' said my father, 'I have a consignment of fine old sherry from Rawlings of St Columb, as you doubtless saw in my cellar-book. A conscientious trader, that Rawlings; I make a point of dealing with him. Yes, we'll have up a bottle or two – and the men shall be entertained meanwhile in the kitchen.'

So my father, quietly enjoying himself, chatted away pleasantly; and after a few glasses of Rawlings' sherry, Tidecombe put off his suspicious reserve. By the end of dinner he and my father were gossiping like a couple of old friends. We heard all Tidecombe's grievances over the difficulties of his job, and the manner in which peasantry and gentry alike were ganged up against him. And about what dolts his men were, and how he was confident he could have laid hands on the contraband last night, had not his men taken to their heels because of a mad woman's cursings. My father was most sympathetic.

'By the way,' said he, 'I've been thinking – there's the spinney beyond the water-meadows. Have you thoroughly searched there?'

Tidecombe admitted that he hadn't thought of it.

'But that's the likeliest place of all!' said my father. 'The undergrowth, you know, very secret. Dick shall lead you there; for it's marshy going if you don't know where to step. And on the way he shall show you our duck pond. I flatter myself it's quite famous. I had it specially built. And my breed of ducks – well, no need to tell you how tender-fleshed *they* are. I'd like to present you with a sitting of eggs; but I imagine – pray correct me if I am wrong – I imagine poultry-keeping is not much in your line?'

So, with a much mollified – indeed, quite sunny-tempered-Tidecombe, and his two grinning underlings, I set off for the oak spinney, on what proved, needless to say, to be an ineffectual search. The ducks were swimming and diving in the sunny waters of the pond as we passed by. Tidecombe admired their fine size and plumage, and praised the ingenious construction of the pond; well raised, as he remarked, to keep the water from seeping out into a bog.

And so back to the stables. And before mounting and riding off, he shook me by the hand and bid me apologize to my father for any unnecessary trouble he might have caused us.

I did feel troubled, but not by Tidecombe. My trouble concerned Kappen's words to me earlier that day. I thought he must have been wanting to warn me in some way – or was it to threaten me? But how could he possibly have discovered the secret of our pond? Had someone been blabbing? No, I couldn't believe it! I wished I could go in and tell my father. But I was too bewildered to devise an appropriate roundabout way of conveying the news to him; and to tell him direct would be an unforgivable impropriety. I felt I must confide in someone, however; and decided that the someone should be Parson Lanyon.

I found him with a veil over his head, and wearing thick gloves, precariously balanced in the fork of an old apple-tree, shaking down an early swarm of bees into a skep which Jimmy Bandy was holding up.

'I want to speak to you, sir,' said I.

'You must wait, Dick, you must wait,' said he. 'Keep your distance now, or you'll get stung. Hold the skep up higher, Jim – bless my soul, one would think you'd never seen me take a swarm before, the way you –'

'It's important,' I said, clapping my hand to my cheek, where an angry bee had just landed.

'Maybe,' said Parson Lanyon. 'But this is more important at the moment.'

I picked the sting out of my cheek, and retreated to the other end of the orchard, flapping at the bees that were buzzing in my hair.

I sat down under the wall and waited, till, the swarm being safe-housed, Parson Lanyon condescended to come down from the tree. Even then he tutted and pished over Jimmy Bandy's clumsiness, and said it was no thanks to him that they hadn't lost the queen. But at last, having read him a little lecture on the humours and antipathies of the tiresome little creatures – for which, at the moment, I myself felt no great liking – he dismissed Jim (who stumped off somewhat dolefully) and came over and let himself down on the grass at my side.

'Well, Dick, what is it?'

I told him of my conversation with Kappen. And he instantly scrambled to his feet again. 'This must be seen into at once!' he exclaimed. 'I don't like it, Dick!'

'Nor do I,' I assured him.

'But I'll wager my wig the man's straight,' said he. 'I have the greatest admiration for him.'

Did I share that admiration? I didn't know. However, I held my tongue.

'Wait here till I've had word with him,' said Parson Lanyon. 'I know where he is. He asked me for a little job – to show his gratitude, as he put it – so I placed a hoe in his hand and sent him to the cabbage patch. Reminding him, of course, not to exert himself unduly.'

Well, well, Parson Lanyon was gone about half an hour,

and came back at a trot, his cheeks pink with his hurrying, and his lips smiling.

He flopped down beside me again. 'It's all right, Dick,' he said, 'no cause for anxiety at all. The man's incapable of guile, as I knew he would be. He told me everything without reserve. In brief, my dear boy, his ears are sharper than a dog's. He heard "sounds in the night"; he was worried for my safety – good fellow! – he dressed and went out. Yes, he dressed and went out, my boy, sick as he was. Think of that! Those sharp ears of his led him to the duck pond; he sensed what was going on; as an old hand in the game himself, he felt you were making more noise than you should: something creaked, something needing oiling, he told me.'

'Then why wasn't he more open with me?' I protested.

'Now, now, Dick, calm yourself. We went thoroughly into that matter. Simplicity itself! How could he distinguish one of you from another in the darkness? How did he know that you were actually there? How could he tell whether you were in the secret or not? He couldn't, my boy! As he truly said, you are scarce more than a child, and perhaps not to be entrusted with such weighty matters. It was cleverly done. If you *were* in the secret, you were warned: if not – well, there you are! We must see to that oiling, Dick; and I'll drop a word in Zach's ear about the need for stricter silence. Now, give me a hand up, there's a good lad, for I seem to have a crick in my back. And put the whole matter out of your mind.'

Comfortable counsel! But I didn't quite succeed in putting the matter out of my mind. For one thing, the distance from the parsonage to the duck pond was near on two miles. How, at that distance, could ears, even 'sharper than a dog's', have heard the small sounds we made? And, for another thing, I felt ruffled at being set down as 'scarce more than a child'. *I*, a great, strapping lad of nearly fifteen! And I found myself hurt that Kappen had not been open with me. Yes, suspicious, hurt, and troubled. But it was no good saying another word about it to Parson Lanyon.

7
The Calling of the Cleeve

The games we had with that Tidecombe! Leading him off on false scents, flashing lights on far-off beaches, and sending him galloping here, there, and everywhere on fruitless searches. Crabbers, landing their lawful hauls, would act for his benefit like guilty thieves; and, after suffering their boats to be searched with a great display of unwillingness, would indignantly threaten to 'have the law on him'. A man loaded his donkey with two heavy tubs, wandered off into the night across Tidecombe's path, was halted, questioned, and detained. But the tubs, when 'rummaged', were found to be filled with sea water 'for the rheumatics'. The man brought his grievance to court, and a hilarious jury awarded him damages.

It was with such enjoyable pranks that the smugglers passed the time in the intervals of their more serious business. With some three hundred miles of wild coast to patrol, and the 'honest thieves' busy in every cove and bay of it, Tidecombe's task was an all but hopeless one. And though he had several times called out the dragoons to his aid, the smugglers knew well whose side the dragoons were on – many of them having an interest in the free trade themselves; and the rest only asking to be entertained with a few free drinks at the nearest ale house.

And try as Tidecombe would to keep his plans and movements secret, the very air itself seemed to bring tidings of them. So, when we learned that he was off to the north coast with half of his men, the duck pond was opened up and the contraband carried across the moors to the central hideout on Trevy Downs. Such of Tidecombe's men as remained among us were easily 'accommodated', as Parson Lanyon would put it. There was a bit of a friendly shindy between us and them in the night on the high moors, with some shooting wide of the mark on either side; a futile attempt to lay hold of a donkey or two, so well trained and so well greased that they were kicking up their heels and off into the darkness before any could get a hand on them; and one decoy beast who led the Excise men at a docile trot to the place of the Standing Stones. Here two tubs of brandy and two sacks of tobacco lay dumped, and not so nicely hidden but that the Excise men could find them, and carry them off in cheering triumph – leaving the rest of the night, and the rest of the moor, at our disposal.

The granite hut among the tin-workings on Trevy Downs was a large one, and a good dozen of the tinners would be sleeping there every night. Great bundles of turves and stacks of furze were piled up in the wood corner beside the big chimney. And behind the turves was a small door, not more than two feet in height: the chimney end was double, and beyond the little door steps led down to a vast cellar. In this cellar any amount of contraband could be safely stored. The hut had no windows, only a few loopholes, where a stone had been left out here and there in the walls to let in air and a glimmer of light. The entrance to the hut itself was low and narrow; so that, altogether, it was a place that a dozen men could hold against a hundred if it came to a fight – but it never had in my memory.

From this central hide-out the goods were gradually carried off, as occasion offered, by the interested – who were, to say truth, most of the population; some portion, of course, having been already disposed of in our own hamlet, at the Pure Drop, and at the parsonage, and in the well at the back of our stableyard.

I couldn't quite have said why, but it did not please me to find Roger Kappen (now fully recovered) busying himself so officiously about the disposal of the contraband in our own hamlet. I had taken a dislike to the man, and could wish now I had never set eyes on him. He had an uncanny way of knowing all about everything; and though Parson Lanyon explained it by his being 'an old hand at the business', it didn't quite explain it to me. He watched the moon, now nearing its full, and predicted the exact date of Zach's next run, when the moon would be waning. And he confidently gave me news of the new Revenue cutter expected at Priddymouth – of which we had heard but the vaguest rumours.

'Cap'n John Hawkhurst,' says he. 'And a terror! If them Jewels ain't fly – he'll nab 'em!'

'Zach would take some nabbing,' I said hotly.

'Aye, boy, I'm not denying of it. But you know what's

said about once too often. Ah, he's a fine fellow, is Zach. A pity, too –'

'*What's* a pity?' I asked, exasperated.

'If we should come to see him one day with a rope about his neck.'

The mere suggestion of such a thing flung me into a fury.

'I'll trouble you to keep your nasty mouth shut!' I cried.

He laughed. 'Now, Dick, don't get your dander up along of me. I'm a proper friend to you, and a proper friend to all your friends. Old Ralph don't fergit you as good as saved his life.'

It was on the tip of my tongue to say that I wished I had left him to die where I had found him. But I knew I couldn't truly wish it. I walked away from him fuming; and it was only after I had cooled down that I remembered he had called himself Ralph and not Roger. Why? Could he be living among us under an assumed name? Well, I would get to the bottom of that! I sought him out again.

'What's your name?' I demanded.

'My name?' says he. 'What now? Ain't I told you my name?'

'Why did you call yourself Ralph just now?'

'Oh,' says he, 'is that what's troubling of 'ee. Can't a man have two names? Roger Ralph Kappen, that's me name. Roger for me dad, and Ralph for me grandad, see? You can call me one, or you can call me t'other – it makes no odds to me. *Now*, be 'ee satisfied?'

Well, I wasn't satisfied – but what could I do? I knew nothing against the man, and yet I suspected that all was not right with him. But suspect what I would, and hint what I would, I could not shake the parson's faith in him.

It was a great relief to me when he took himself out of

the hamlet. Where our rough grazing land ended and the moor began there was an empty thatched cottage standing in a small croft: a wan-looking little place enough, but more or less weathertight. The walls, of unhewn moor-stones, had been raised in a long summer's night by some tinner or other; for it was a law with us that what a man could build on unused ground between sunset and sunrise he could claim as his own. So the tinner had lived and died there in the house of his own making; and since then the place had stood empty. In this cottage Parson Lanyon now installed his protégé, offering to pay a shilling or two's rent for it out of his own pocket – rent which my father amused himself by agreeing to, and always refusing.

Parson Lanyon bought the fellow a horse, too, to plough up the croft and draw sand and seaweed for manuring. A great, lumbering, heavy-footed animal it was, and black as a crow, for since Kappen said he fancied that colour and size, the parson went to no end of trouble to get him just what he wanted. My father raised his eyebrows; but, beyond remarking dryly how fortune was apt to favour those who least deserved it, made no protest. And as for myself, I would willingly have searched the county for any coloured horse – blue, red, white, or spotted – provided that it kept Kappen at a distance from me.

He moved into his new quarters just before the May gale. In our part of the country we could always expect a gale in May, and a bugbear it was to us, blighting the early potatoes as like as not, and nipping the fruit buds just when everything was showing such fair promise. But the gale we had this May I am telling of was the worst I can recall at that time of the year. And, to herald it, came a sound not often heard: a sound that the fisherfolk called the 'calling of the cleeve'.

The weather was sultry, and I had been out to sea with Zach in the morning, laying crab pots. We had just come ashore, and were going up the cliff path, when there fell a most strange silence over the land. Not a bird chirped, not a dog barked, not a leaf stirred. And though the sun was blazing, it felt to me as if the world had gone dark.

'Hark!' said Zach, holding up his hand. 'Hear it, boy?'

I did hear it – all along the sun-glittering line of cliffs: a low rumble, dying away to a sigh, returning again to a heavy mutter, rising about us, enveloping us, as it were, in an indistinct threat of sound that was neither of the sea nor of the land, where all was quiet. It was as if the very cliffs themselves, after aeons of silence, had suddenly found a voice and were grumbling at the hardness of their lot.

'Cleeves calling,' said Zach. 'There's a heavy storm on the way.'

'But where, but *how,* Zach?' I asked, bewildered, for I had not heard that sound before.

'I can't tell 'ee how, son, but *where* is out there to the sou'westard. Aye, the storm's out there, right enough, and the cliffs have caught the echo of it, though how 'tis carried to 'em beats me. But you an' me'll get us down to Cove agin, and haul up the *Mayfly* high's we can, or she'll be in splinters afore night, I shouldn't wonder. Maybe you best nip up and call t'others. But no need, they've heard, and they'm coming.'

I looked up and saw Harry and Job and Matthy coming down towards us at a run.

'We've lost our pots, boys, that's sartin sure,' said Zach.

'Go after 'em, shan't us?' said Job.

'Nay, us'll leave 'em be,' said Zach. 'Better lost pots than lost lives.' For Zach, though bold as any lion, was never foolhardy.

It seemed absurd, with scarce a ripple on the water! The cliffs had resumed their age-old silence now, and the small birds were chirruping again. Though I noticed that the gulls were rising from the rocks and flying inland.

'I can't believe there's going to be a storm!' I said.

'There's going to be such a storm, boy, as maybe you've never seen,' Zach assured me. 'The cleeves don't call for naught.'

We emptied the *Mayfly* of her gear, and carried sails, oars, ropes, and everything movable up into the highest of the caves. Then it came to the turn of the boat herself. Far back at the end of the deepest cave, whose floor sloped upward to the entrance of the tunnel I spoke of earlier, there was a rusty little winch and a length of tackle. By means of this tackle, with two of us straining at the winch, and the rest of us keeping the *Mayfly* on an even keel, we got her over the flat rocks under the jetty. But when it came to the steep shingle beyond the rocks, our task was a heavy one. However, by shoving and using rollers, we had her up at last, the winch all the time keeping a rattling accompaniment to our panting breath.

'Now may the Lord in His mercy spare her!' exclaimed Matthy, who had lately joined the Methodists, and was full of pious sentiments. And with that, down he flopped on his knees on the floor of the cave, and put up a fervent prayer for the preservation of the *Mayfly*; while Harry muttered, 'You may as well stow that guff!' and the rest of us stood by in embarrassed silence.

'Guff?' said Matthy, rising from his knees. 'And if the Lord takes her – where's our livelihood? What about our next run? What about them tubs bought and paid for over to Roscoff? What about –'

'Oh, well,' said Zach, 'what is to be, will be, I s'pose.

And you best be off home, Dick boy, and give warning of what's to come.'

There was no need to give warning. The storm burst in a sudden fury before I was half-way home. Before I knew what was happening, I was lifted off my feet and blown over a low stone wall. I picked myself up and ran on, the wind whirling my coat tails about my ears, and the world about me now as full of noise as it had been empty before. Every bush was screaming, every stunted tree groaning and clapping its boughs; the grass and bracken at my feet twisted and hissed like a nest of serpents, and at my back the sea roared and the spume flew over my head.

When I got home I found everyone in a rare bustle, and my father, with an old muffler tied over his hat, riding hither and thither, shouting orders against the racket of the wind. He was a man of action now, with his brows drawn down over his piercing eyes, his bony jaw set in firm lines, and all his superciliousness dropped from him. I got my orders with the rest of the men, and was immediately on Diamond and galloping up to the pastures to help round up the sheep and lambs. Others of us were bringing in cows and calves, yet others stabling the brood mares, while those horses that were left to fend for themselves bucked and flung up their heels and went careering across the meadows, neighing shrilly. Meanwhile, clouds like toppling mountains came driving in from the sea, blackening the sky, bringing rain that fell in torrents; and all the time every inanimate thing found a voice and gave tongue, with a clapping of wood and rattling of iron and groaning and clattering of gates and doorways. The roofs of our barns and outhouses were well secured against just such emergencies with a lashing of chains clamped to heavy stones; but I saw one roof, where the chains must have partially rusted through, suddenly rise into the air and go flying away inland as if on wings. Right glad I was to get indoors, where the women had been round closing windows and bolting shutters; right glad I was to get out of my soaking clothes, and sit warm and dry, though with ringing ears and a dazed mind, in front of a blazing log fire.

'The tinners be out along the cliffs in their hundreds,' said old Nathaniel, coming in with the hot rum toddy my father had ordered.

'A vessel sighted?' asked my father, getting quickly to his feet.

'Nay,' said Nathaniel. 'Not yet, but hopes of one.'

8
The Wreck

All that day, and all through the night, the gale raged without pause. The next morning, Sunday, Parson Lanyon put up a heartfelt prayer – shouting it full-voiced against the howl of the wind through the church – for those 'that go down to the sea in ships, that do business in great waters'.

The church was full, as it always was, whatever the

weather, for we were a God-fearing community, except for the tinners. The time was to come, and that very shortly, when the tinners in their multitudes would be sitting at the feet of the sainted John Wesley. But, just now, they were greeting him with howls of abuse and showers of stones whenever he came among them, and they usually spent their Sundays at the ale house. Though, on this morning, they were strung out all along the cliffs on the look-out for the hoped-for wreck.

'O gracious God and loving Father,' prayed Parson Lanyon, 'spare the lives of those who put their trust in Thee. But, O most merciful God, if in Thine inscrutable wisdom Thou hast decided that a ship shall be wrecked, let it, we beseech Thee, be wrecked upon this coast, for the benefit of the poor inhabitants.'

The whole congregation breathed a fervent 'Amen' to the conclusion of this prayer, but nobody paid much attention to anything else that the parson might say. The most of us were fidgeting in our seats, and turning our heads round towards the door at every louder boom of wind. And when that door was flung open with a clap that sent the hanging lamps crazily swinging, everybody leaped to their feet.

'A wreck – a wreck on Garrick Sands!' the whisper went round. And there was a rush for the door.

'Andy!' bellowed Parson Lanyon, banging with his fist on the pulpit rail, 'shut home that door!'

At the tremendous voice of authority the rush for the outer air was momentarily halted, and the congregation stood irresolute. Andy slammed the door. Parson Lanyon, snatching off his surplice, hopped out of the pulpit and pushed his way to the back of the church.

'Now' – cried he, as he flung the door open – 'now, my Christian brethren, we'll all start fair!'

And off he raced into the storm, with the whole congregation, men, women, and children, pelting after him.

He was soon left behind by the more active, and I found myself, rather reluctantly, clutched by the arm and dragging him along. Trees were crashing about us in the valley, the stream was a raging torrent, flecked with the spume of the sea, and in the roar and tumult we couldn't have heard ourselves speak even if we had breath to do so. And as we neared the shore the blown sand came against us like a shower of hail.

The sands, down to the very edge of the great breakers, were black with people, darting this way and that, gesticulating, shouting with unheard voices. And beyond the breakers a large schooner lay on her side, heaving and rolling like an animal in its death agony, amid a strew of torn canvas and broken spars. Men were clinging to the rigging and clustered like ants on the bowsprit, men were tossing in the sea, flinging up their arms in a struggle which could have but one end. I saw a crowded ship's boat, caught among the breakers, leap like a crazed thing from the water, fall again, heel over, shake herself free of her living load, and come driving inshore, rolling over and over like a monstrous cork.

A few poor souls were dragged out of the breakers by a chain of willing hands; for though we were all wreckers at heart, and though to save a man from the sea was accounted unlucky among us, yet we were not heartless, and I know that the tears shed by the watching women – aye, and by some of the men, too – were tears of genuine pity, even though at the back of everyone's mind must have lurked an eager anticipation of coming spoils. For myself, I was wrought up into a pitch of wild excitement, in which shudderings of horror and an intoxicating sense of the awfulness of the scene were about equally blended.

'I'm taking a rope out!' shouted a familiar voice beside me.

'No such thing you bain't, Zach!' yelled Methodist Matthy.

I have said that Zach was not foolhardy, and maybe I should take back those words. For what but foolhardiness – or the heroism that resembles it – possessed him now? And now the whole appalling catastrophe narrowed itself for me into the figure of one man – and that man my hero! – in a life and death struggle with the fury of the waves. I saw him, with a rope under his armpits, dive headlong into the breakers, saw him washed under, flung up, dragged back to shore by those who held the rope, heard the expostulations, the shouts that bid him desist, saw him venture again, fail again, be dragged back again. I was sobbing now, and babbling out frantic prayers, all unconscious that the rope, of which I, too, had a hold, was tearing the skin from my bleeding hands.

'God, if you let him drown, I will never forgive you, in this world or the next!' I shrieked.

God did not let Zach drown. He was through those breakers at last, and the wind whirled away the tremendous cheer that we sent up as we saw him dragged aboard the schooner by the men who leaned out over the dipping bowsprit. Clinging to that rope, many of the crew were able to get ashore, though some, struck senseless by the weight of the pounding breakers, relaxed their hold, and were washed out to sea again.

In all, nineteen of the crew landed living on the sands, though some scarce breathing, and many injured, and with broken bones. When at last Zach stood once more at my side, my thanks to God were as heartfelt as my recent threats had been; though my eyes, blinded by the whirl of the stinging sand, and maybe also by tears, could see nothing clearly. And I scarce noticed that Zach held, gripped about the body, the unconscious form of a yellow-haired lad of about my own age.

9

A 'Bad Un'?

It is one thing to save men from drowning; it is quite another thing to restore them their property. In the howling billows of ocean all proprietary rights are washed away and what comes from the sea is for those who gather it – that was the firm conviction of us all. The survivors having been led or carried up to the hamlet, given shelter in the manor and parsonage, resuscitated, warmed and fed by a group of the women, the serious business of helping ourselves to all that the sea had brought us began in earnest.

The Dutch schooner carried a mixed cargo, and a rich one: bales of silk, ribbons, and threadbone lace, embroidered waistcoats and gold and silver brocade from Italy; printed calicoes from France, packages of cocoa and chocolate from Holland, together with a goodly chest full of smuggled dollars from Spain. As the tide ebbed, these spoils lay strewn along the whole length of Garrick Sands, among the smashed wreckage of the ship herself – spars, planks, sailcloth, cordage, broken furniture, bedding, and seamen's clothing. It was from under the sodden remnants of a straw mattress that I picked up the round-bellied ship's lantern that now hangs over our great doorway and sheds such a cheering light out into the blackness of winter nights. The lamp is so constructed that it flings out more greatly magnified beams the farther you are from it, so that from the end of the park it shines like an immense friendly beacon welcoming you home. I had never seen such a lantern before, and I treasured it more than anything else I garnered from the sands that day.

Meanwhile, in their hundreds – not only from our parish but from all the surrounding country – men, women, and children were gathering their spoils into heaps, heaps that once placed, it was understood, no one else had the right to touch. Nor did anyone touch them, lest there be murder done, such was our recognized code of fair dealing. As it was, there was fighting enough, with blows and cursing and heavy tussling among the men, and pulling and scratching and screaming among the women, whenever two or three happened to lay hold of the same piece of salvage at one and the same moment. But Parson Lanyon, thrusting his way among the angry combatants, was usually able to make the peace, his roaring voice of authority silencing even the most bellicose. His own share of the spoils, as far as I could see, was no more than one

silk bandana – and that tattered; for though the joy of wrecking was like wine in his blood, he cared far more for the 'benefit of the poor inhabitants' than for his own gain. And I saw him, not once, but many times, slyly adding a contribution to the pile of a poor old hobbling widow, who could do little for herself.

The gale, having done its worst, was dying away; and when the sands lay bare with the full ebb of the tide, the tinners, armed with sharp axes, waded through the shal-

lows to the wrecked schooner, and hacked to pieces what remained of her. While they were so occupied, who should make his belated arrival, but 'stinking great Tidecombe' and his gang! But the tinners turned upon him in a body, and chased him off the beach, his men ignoring his repeated orders to use their guns.

It was only, I'm afraid, when the sands were completely cleared of wreckage, that any thought was given to the dead. As I heard one man remark to another, 'Let 'em bide where they be for a while; us can do nothing for they.'

'No, poor worms, more's the pity,' said the other.

It was not till next morning that these dead, both whole bodies, and what the parson described as 'gobbets', were covered with sailcloths, carried up to the churchyard, and there buried in a common grave. Parson Lanyon shed tears over the burial service, and prayed for all our sins to be forgiven us; and, when the earth had been shovelled back over the dead, he ordered the living to betake themselves to the Pure Drop, there to be generously refreshed at his expense.

During the next few days Doctor Treglown was busy among the survivors, both up at the manor and down at the parsonage; and as they recovered they were sent on their way, each with a goodly bundle of food and a sufficiency of money, subscribed by any of us who had a farthing to spare. The Dutch captain, who could speak English, protested vigorously and oathfully about the seizure of his cargo, but nobody heeded him. Indeed, he hadn't a leg to stand on, since most of his cargo was contraband: the importation of silks, embroidery, chocolate, cocoa, printed calicoes, ribbons and laces, gloves and mittens, being prohibited by law under any circumstances whatsoever. When blown off his course by the gale, he had been making for Priddymouth, we understood; and in that lawless port such cargoes were habitually landed under the very noses of the port officials, who were at that time, before the coming of Captain John Hawkhurst, powerless against a whole town full of armed rebels.

The last of the crew to recover was the yellow-haired lad whom Zach had brought ashore in his arms. Nobody seemed to know anything about him. When questioned, the Dutch captain shrugged up his massive shoulders and said, 'Call him Neil. Pick him up on quay. Vork vell, but say noddings. Maybe cannot speak, ha?'

'But he is not a deaf mute,' said Doctor Treglown; 'he can hear as well as I can.'

To which the captain shrugged again, and said, 'Know nodding.'

It was true, the lad never said one word. But it was also true, as Doctor Treglown had said, that he could hear as well as anybody. His shipmates having all departed, my father, not knowing what else to do with him, decided to keep him, and, when he was able, set him to help our farm man. It fell to my lot to teach him the names of things in English, and to befriend him generally. I couldn't make him out. Sometimes he would smile, but sometimes there would come into his eyes a wild expression, as if he were looking upon something most terrible. Well, he had suffered shipwreck, and I supposed that accounted for it; but it seemed to me to show a lack of spirit in him, giving me, I regret to admit, a pleasant sense of my own superiority. Also he sometimes irritated me. 'I believe you can speak well enough if you want to,' I once said to him. 'Why don't you? It's too stupid, the way you go on!'

But he only gave me a strange look, and shook his head.

There was one thing he seemed to share with me: an instinctive dislike of Roger Kappen. I shall never forget the first time those two met. It was early evening, and Neil and I were coming out of the churchyard (where we had been playing a game of fives against the tower wall) when we came face to face with Kappen, with his black horse and sledge, going down to the shore for a load of sea sand.

'You and I be most strangers, Dick,' says he. 'And who have you got there?'

'It's –' I began. But Neil, after one long stare into Kappen's face, took to his heels.

'Well,' says Kappen, turning to watch Neil's running figure, 'that's a funny caper! Is he totelling [crazy] or what?'

'No,' said I, 'he's sane enough. But he's kind of scared, since Zach saved him from the wreck.'

'Oh, so Zach saved him from the wreck, did he?' says Kappen. 'One of them Hollanders, eh? But I reckon he'll speak our lingo?'

'He doesn't seem to be able to speak at all, in any language,' I said.

'Not speak?' said Kappen. 'What next? But he'll write a tidy hand, I shouldn't wonder?'

I said he couldn't write, either in Dutch or English, or read, as far as I could make out. But that I was hoping to teach him his letters.

Kappen laughed, spat on the turf, and remarked that foreigners 'was mostly trash'. 'Don't you set no store by the likes of he, Dick,' he said, 'nor trouble yourself to learn him naught. The likes of he have no proper feelings in their hearts, by what I can make out of it. The likes of he'll toady up to you one day, and cut your throat the next.'

'What are you talking about?' I said hotly, 'Neil's a nice lad!'

'A nice lad, is he?' said Kappen thoughtfully. 'Well, that's as may be. But if I know bad from good, that lad's a bad un.'

'What utter rubbish!' I cried, and was turning on my heel when Kappen stopped me.

'I've a word more yet,' he began slowly. 'Now see here, Dick, you've took agin me, I know. And I'm not faulting you for that. Young lads takes notions into their heads for little reason. 'Tis that Doctor Treglown have set you agin me, I reckon. But because I'm not so pretty-looking as some, it don't mean that my heart ain't right. And like me or not, I'm your friend, Dick, and would do anything for 'ee, as one day you'll know. And as to that lad, don't say I haven't warned 'ee. But I can't stay courseying here, 'bout him nor naught else. I'm busy, I am. Kim 'ip with 'ee, Colonel!'

And so, with a pull on the rope reins, he set his big-footed horse in motion, and took himself off, the sledge bumping and creaking over the rough ground.

Well, I didn't know what to make of all that. I felt uncomfortable that Kappen should have sensed my dislike of him. And that made me wonder if the parson was right about him, and myself perhaps just a silly goose. Perhaps those few words of Doctor Treglown's *had* prejudiced me against him? I didn't want to be unjust to anyone. But, all the same, it seemed to me that Kappen was being unjust towards Neil, who, I felt sure, was harmless enough.

In this somewhat bewildered state of mind I went to look for Neil. After a long search, I found him hidden behind the wood pile by our kitchen door. He came out reluctantly. And when I spoke to him of Kappen, he turned his head aside, and gestured with his hand, as if he were pushing something horrid away from him. An hour ago I should have been pleased to find him sharing my opinion of Kappen. But now, with Kappen's words fresh in my memory, I caught myself wondering whether it was he who had seen through Kappen or Kappen who had seen through him. Oh, what did it matter? And, anyway, there was one thing I did feel: that Neil was a great softy for running away like that – my own opinion, instilled into me by Zach Jewel, being that when you met with anything you feared or mistrusted, you should never run away, but, on the contrary, 'draw nigh to it'.

'For if you take and run from it, boy,' Zach had once assured me, 'it'll be after 'ee, and stick in your mind like any plague, that's sartin sure.'

10

Adventure at the Angel

Zach was courting a girl called Janey Keigwin, the landlady's pretty daughter at the Angel Inn in Venton. The drink sold at the Angel was, of course, all of the smuggled variety – for how else could Mrs Anne Keigwin make a living? Why should she pay the Government 4*s*. a gallon for port, and 8*s*. 6*d*. for brandy, when she could get it from Zach at 2*s*. and 3*s*. 6*d*.? And who among her customers but would go elsewhere if she charged them at such an exorbitant rate?

Now Zach, having made another successful run, proposed paying a visit to the Angel, to deliver Mrs Anne Keigwin's standing order in person, and to see his sweetheart, Janey. I offered him my cob, Diamond, for the trip, in return for being allowed to go with him; and we set out on a merry June morning, Diamond harnessed to a ramshackle cart of Zach's, the cart packed with the tubs of wine and spirit, and the tubs covered with a tarpaulin. Under the tarpaulin, also, Zach had put a jar of butter, a bowl of eggs, and three wild ducks and a hare he had shot, as gifts for Mrs Keigwin. For Janey he carried, wrapped in a square of new sailcloth in his coat pocket, a bunch of gay ribbons and some lace, which he had saved for her from the wreck.

So, on a windless morning, we trundled our way across the heath behind Jewel's Place. That heath was a dreary place enough in winter; but today it gave you a joyous feeling just to look at it, dressed as it was in all its early

summer bravery of small starry flowers: sea pink and golden tormentil, squills blue as the sea, and rosy rock-spurry, and a flame of gorse that filled the air with sweetness, and resounded with the sharp *chack-chack* of red-breasted stonechats.

Zach beguiled the way with tales of sea adventures, and descriptions of Roscoff, where, he said, so many smugglers with a price on their heads had settled that the rents of houses and stores had risen amazingly. And they had their own chapel there, being most of them converted to Methodism.

'Aye,' says he, 'if it ever comes to brother Matthy's turn to spend a term of hiding overseas, he'll find himself proper at home in Roscoff!'

'If he sticks to you he'll never have the need,' I said, so great was my faith in Zach's skill and cunning.

Zach chuckled and said you could never be sure, what with things tightening up, and this Captain John Hawkhurst already taken over at Priddymouth.

'He was after us last trip,' said Zach; 'aye, and come up with us, too. A near go that was. But we sank the tubs just in time, and had the good luck to overhaul a crabber from down west'ard, and changed gear with him, none too soon. So when this Hawkhurst come up with us, there was naught but crabs in the boat. Mighty suspicious he was, though, sniffing here, and snuffing there, and we boys with our pipes all going to account for the smell of baccy. And I'm thinking us'll do best to launch out in a bigger way. So I've pledged my mind to get me a handsome little lugger, crew of, say, twenty-five, and as many guns. Then if it comes to a scrap us can hold our own.'

'Oh, Zach, take me on as one of the crew – do, *please*!' I urged.

'Nay, nay,' said Zach laughing, 'you know I can't do that.'

I was so eager that I told him I would risk my father's displeasure, even if it meant absconding from home. Whereat Zach became serious and told me I mustn't talk that way.

'Squire's a rare good man,' said he, 'and I wouldn't vex him for the world.'

He was serious, too, on the subject of Tidecombe. For it seemed that Tidecombe had somehow got wind that there was a hide-out on Trevy Downs, and had been seen by a tinner nosing round up there one dark night. Not that he'd found anything.

'And a good job he didn't,' said Zach, 'or he wouldn't have lived to tell the tale. But what vexes me is how he come to be up there at all. There's not one in the seven parishes would sell him the secret for all the gold in the kingdom.'

'It must have been one of his own men,' I said. And I reminded him of the amiable scrap we had had with them on the night we carried up the gear.

'If I thought that,' said Zach, 'there'd be no more presents left lying about handy for the likes of they scurvy dogs ... Aye, but I s'pose you must be right, boy. Anyways we're quit of Tidecombe for the time being. He come a crack in the dark agin a moorstone, same as the old woman wished him. And now he's laid up with a broken leg, so they say.'

'Do you really believe Gracie Winkey has all that power, Zach?' I asked.

'Believe it?' said Zach. ' 'Course I believe it! How come Tidecombe to fall off his hoss if not through she?'

I thought there might be other reasons, but I didn't say so. And so, talking of many things, we crossed over the heath, and came out at last on to the turnpike road, and into Venton, and up the steep street to the Angel.

Zach bid me wait in a doorway down the street, while he drove the cart into the coaching-yard at the back of the Angel. I asked him why, and he said he wasn't 'taking no chances'. And when I asked him *what* chances, he said you never knew who was about.

'You stay where you be, and count five hundred slow,' he said. 'And then walk round to the yard by the alley at the back, and in through the little gate. I'll be waiting for 'ee.'

I chafed at all this, thinking it absurd, but he was right, as it happened. So I counted my five hundred, and then walked up the alley and came in at the back of the yard, and found Zach waiting for me. But still he wasn't taking chances. He bid me wait by the cart, while he went to the kitchen door to 'spy out the land'. I kept my eye on the door, and saw him cautiously push it open and step into the shadowed passage. I heard his low whistle, and a flurry of light answering steps and the swish of petticoats, and Zach's soft laugh as he kissed his Janey and put his hand in his pocket to bring out his little present for her. Then there was a moment's whispering, and Zach came out again and walked quickly over to the cart.

'Of all the ill-wisht nuisances!' he muttered. 'There's searchers in the bar. No, not Tidecombe – of course, he's quiet enough – but a fellow from Priddymouth – told you things was tightening up! Howsomever, he knows the cut of my jib, seemingly, having been with Hawkhurst t'other day, which won't make him the less anxious to catch me tripping now.'

'We best get away quick, then?' I whispered.

'*What?*' said Zach. 'Come all this way and turn tail for a parcel of Priddymouth hoddyman-doddies? And me and Janey not had our speak out nor nothing? Not if I knows it! Now look 'ee here, boy. They seen me come in. They was peeking from bar window. But they ain't seen you. And me and you ain't acquainted, see? You do as I say, now. In that there shed there's a box hearse, and in that there stable there's a moke. You get them tubs out the cart and into the hearse, and harness the moke up to it. But leave the few bits of presents for Anne Keigwin – the eggs and that – in the cart, and fasten the tarpaulin tight down over 'em, mind you. And when you hears me laugh loud from the bar, drive the hearse slow and steady out the yard, and past the bar windows. If a black-cloaked female should join up with you, that'll be Janey. When you get so far as Badgery Lane, nip in and ask James Cody to let you put the hearse in his store. You'll do all that?'

'Why, yes,' I said, 'but –'

'Ain't no buts about it,' said Zach.

And off he strode, whistling a tune and stamping his feet. And the kitchen door closed behind him.

He told me about it afterwards. So now you may picture him clattering merrily into the bar, with his loud 'Good morning, gentlemen all'; winking at Anne Keigwin, standing a round of drinks to everyone, and then another round and still another; asking for news, giving news, talking loud and hearty, acting simple, cracking foolish jokes, telling colourful stories, while the young officer from Priddymouth smiled to himself, biding his time; and his men, half-seas over with the drinks, baited him and led him on, amusing themselves at his expense, as they thought. A foolish bird caught in a snare, as they must have considered him.

Till at last, feigning drunkenness himself, he became confidential, and the young officer pricked up his ears. Oh yes, simple-minded Zach Jewel would tell them all he knew about the smugglers – 'mentioning no names, of course, gentlemen; couldn't expect a man to give away his fellows. But there'll be rare goings-on two nights from now, and that I *do* know. And I wouldn't say but that if you was to pay a visit to such a place and such a place' –

(mentioning places where no smuggler would dream of landing) – 'well, it's not for me to tell no tales, but I wouldn't say but what you mightn't come off lucky.'

And then, all of a sudden, out rings his great laugh, echoing through the bar and drifting out to me in the yard. Meanwhile, I had been feverishly getting the tubs into the box hearse, and harnessing in the moke. I was wildly excited, but I must admit to a slight quailing of the stomach as, at the sound of that laugh, I took the moke by the rein and led it, drawing the hearse, out of the yard and through the archway into the front of the Angel. In the archway a woman was waiting for me. She had a black hood over her head and a handkerchief to her eyes, and she was wrapped in a ragged black cloak that fell to her heels. Humped up inside that cloak, her figure looked bent and old, and I shouldn't have recognized her, but that for a moment she drew aside the handkerchief and looked at me with merry eyes – *Janey!* She laid a warning forefinger against her pursed-up lips, covered her bowed face with the handkerchief again, and gave a most convincing sob. And so, I at the moke's head, and she hanging on to the back of the hearse, and shaking with feigned sobs and little trills of genuine laughter, we passed slowly up the street.

The bar window was thrown up and half a dozen heads thrust out.

'What's coming now?' said a voice.

'A pauper, by the looks of it, being carried up to the bone-yard,' answered another voice.

'His turn today, ours tomorrow, gentlemen.' That was Zach's voice.

I kept my head down and walked on, hearing from the window gusts of half-drunken laughter, with Zach's laugh ringing louder than the rest.

And then, for Zach, came the tricky moment, as he told me later. The young officer suddenly squared his shoulders and became businesslike.

'Zachariah Jewel, for such I understand to be your name,' says he with a conceited smile, 'thanking you I'm sure for entertaining us, and all that – but now to business. You were seen to drive into the inn yard a while back with a covered cart.'

'Oh, a covered cart, is it?' says Zach, acting stupid.

'Useless to attempt denying it,' says the officer. 'I have a search-warrant.'

'Who says I'm denying it?' says Zach, indignant now. 'I'm not denying no such thing! But if a man can't carry a few bits of presents to his poor old grandma what lives top of the town – by name Betty Biggin, she is; and if he can't tarry to refresh hisself among friends on his way – well, what I wants to know is, what's the country coming to? You has your warrant, you say? All right now: you can search my cart and you can search my pockets – you and your warrant – for all that I do care! But it's no free country where a poor man is treated so, and that I'll swear.'

They did search his pockets, and Zach kept them as slow about it as he could, to give me time to reach Badgery Lane. Then, with a great show of reluctance, he went out with them into the yard. Slowly he fumbled with the fastenings of the tarpaulin, till the officer, getting impatient, threatened to slash if off with his sword; at which Zach dared him to damage a poor man's property. And so, after some hot words on both sides, off comes the tarpaulin at last. And there in the cart is nothing but the jar of butter, the bowl of eggs, the three wild ducks, and the hare.

'Is that all now, gentlemen?' says Zach. 'Because, if so,

I'll be going about my business. And I reckon it's time you was going about yours – that is, if you has any, which I rather misdoubt.'

So we diddled the searchers. And when the chagrined young officer had marched his little band of tipsy men out of town, we brought the tubs back to the Angel, helped Anne Keigwin and Janey to store them in the cellar, and then sat down, the four of us, to a merry meal.

II

The Little Peter

Soon after this Zach got his new lugger. He had her especially built for him over at Roscoff. And, since the actual buying of her was all above board and legal, my father made no objection to my taking the trip across channel with the Jewels to fetch her.

That was a proud trip for me. And my pride reached its zenith when I asked Zach her name, for he answered that he would leave the naming of her to me. I then and there christened her the *Little Peter,* which is our name for the storm-petrel. For, as she lifted buoyantly to the wave, and so sweetly and easily glissaded down into the trough, and up again, and down again, gliding on at such speed, yet with no fuss, it seemed to me that her actions were exactly like that little bird's – swift without hurry, and confident in whatever storm.

Yes, the *Little Peter* was a beauty; but, though the profits Zach could now make on each run were far greater, the risks he ran were far greater also. No longer could he and his brothers pose as poor and honest crabbers; they must now become licensed traders, carrying outward-bound cargoes of potatoes and grain from Priddymouth or St Mewes, and returning with legitimate cargoes of building bricks, oranges, butter, and the like. And perhaps, on the whole, the acquiring of the *Little Peter* was an ill-starred venture; though, with a trusty crew of picked men, there seemed no reason why she should come to grief.

It seemed to me that all the fit men in our end of the county were eager to join the crew of the *Little Peter.* And from the volunteers Zach took his pick quickly and decisively. Young fellows they were mostly, and the greater number of them fishermen, bred to the sea since childhood. But there were, too, a few of the neighbouring gentry's sons, scarcely grown men, but older than myself, and with fathers more amenable to reason than mine. Fathers, moreover, who put money into the venture, and so made it easy for Zach to purchase his legitimate cargoes. (I never discovered whether my own father subscribed anything, but most like he did.) Among the crew there were also one or two middle-aged men; men who had hitherto been making runs on their own; and these, as Zach put it, added solid ballast to his company.

It did not please me when I found that Roger Kappen had volunteered, and that Parson Lanyon was urging Zach to take him on.

'Where could you find a better man for the job?' the parson had said. 'The strength of ten, the soul of honour, and an old hand – knowing the business from A to Z. And he deserves a bit of luck to make up for the way those villains treated him.'

'But you're not taking him, are you, Zach?' I asked anxiously.

'Well, no, boy, I'm not,' said Zach. 'Though it irks me to say no to Parson. And, mind you, I know naught agin the man. But then, you see, I know naught *for* him neither. He's a stranger, as you might say, and strangers be right enough in their place. But their place ain't in my boat.'

How relieved I was! And yet I should have been hard put to it to say why. For, like Zach, I knew nothing against Kappen. Only I couldn't forget that remark of Kappen's about seeing a rope about Zach's neck. It made me feel hot with anger every time I thought of it.

Of course, Kappen was not pleased with Zach's refusal. I tried to keep out of his way; but one evening, when I was down by the stream tickling trout, I saw him, out of the corner of my eye, coming up through the valley. He was carrying a gun, and he had three or four rabbits he had shot, tied by the feet and slung across his shoulder.

I stooped over the stream as if I had not seen him, but he came over and stood by my side.

'Well, Dick,' says he, 'I'm thinking of calling in at your place. Maybe Squire would buy a rabbit or two off a poor man?'

'I dare say he would,' says I, with my eyes on the water.

'Aye, a poor man,' repeated Kappen. 'And with fortune snatched out of my hand, in a manner of speaking. You didn't happen to put in a word for me with Zach Jewel, I'm thinking, Dick? For it seems I ain't to be one of the crew.'

'It's nothing to do with me,' I said uncomfortably. 'Zach makes up his own mind; he wouldn't heed anything *I* said.'

'Maybe he wouldn't,' answered Kappen. 'But you know, Dick, I has my feelings; and maybe them feelings is hurt along of you.'

'I'm sorry for that,' I said, not quite truthfully.

'But, mind you, Dick, I'm yer friend through thick and thin.'

Why did the man keep telling me he was my friend? It made me feel awkward, as if somehow I was wronging him in my mind. 'You can have these, if you like,' I said, giving him the two trout I had caught.

'And that's kind of you, Dick,' said he. 'And how's you and yon Hollander getting on?'

'Oh, all right,' I said.

'Speak yet, does he?'

'No,' I said.

'And most like never will,' said Kappen. 'But his writing, what you was teaching of him, he'll be coming along with that?'

'Well,' I said, 'he knows his letters, but that's about all. He doesn't seem very anxious to learn.'

To tell truth, I hadn't been bothering very much about Neil's education. I found it uphill work; and when he gazed at me with that look of fright in his round blue eyes, I put him down for a zany and got impatient.

'Not anxious to learn?' said Kappen. 'That's strange, that is. And you so willing to teach! I'm thinking, Dick, if you was to offer to learn *me* my letters, I'd make shift to learn – out of gratitood, like.'

Oh dear! What was I to say now? 'I – I haven't much time,' I countered.

'No,' agreed Kappen. 'You be always busy, bain't 'ee, what with one thing and another. And that's what makes it all the kinder of 'ee, Dick, to waste your time on that there foreign trash.'

'I really ought to be getting home now,' I said. 'I have some – errands to do for my father.'

What errands? If he asked, what could I answer? But fortunately he didn't ask. He insisted, though, on walking with me as far as the manor. And all the time he was talking about the *Little Peter*, praising her extravagantly – her shape and grace and capacity for speed, and how cunningly she was built for the concealing of contraband. He had every detail of that lugger at his finger-tips; it puzzled me, and I wondered uneasily how he should know so much about her.

'Did Zach show you over her, then?' I asked.

'No need for that,' says he. 'I've got eyes in me head, haven't I? An old free-trader's eyes, Dick, what can take the measure of a craft by looking, whether it be outside or inside, or the difference atween 'em.' He laughed. 'But your secrets is safe with Roger Kappen.'

I hoped indeed that they were. For it was true, as he said the *Little Peter* was cunningly built for the carrying of contraband. She had a double bottom, and double bow and stern; the bunks in the cabin had false bottoms, and the gaily papered ceiling of that cabin had a cavity above it for the storing of silks and muslins; and even the masts and yards were hollow. On her homeward journeys, too, she always carried extra hawsers, and the inner strands of these hawsers were made, not of manilla, but of tobacco. As for the wine and spirit tubs, they were still usually towed, every barrel being provided by the Roscoff merchants with a pair of sling-ropes. These slings were then attached to a long rope weighted with stones. So that all you had to do in an emergency was to fix a heavy anchor on the towing rope, fling it overboard, take your bearings and make off swiftly – to return again when all was safe, and pull up the whole 'crop' with a grapple.

Zach had another idea: to construct a flat-bottomed towing-raft, which would be full of holes, so that when loaded with tubs, it, and they, would be completely submerged. I thought the idea a brilliant one, but the raft never got made; perhaps because so many things kept happening that Zach had no time to attend to it.

What with Tidecombe laid by with his broken leg, all should have been fair sailing for the *Little Peter* that summer, had it not been for the new captain of the Customs cutter at Priddymouth, John Hawkhurst. Perhaps I ought to explain that there were two separate forces engaged in the attempt to put down smuggling. There were the riding-officers to patrol the land, and the Customs cutters to patrol the sea. The last captain of the cutter at Priddymouth had given no one any trouble. To augment his salary, which was none too good, and 'for the sake of his wife and family', as he had once explained to Zach, he did quite a bit in the smuggling line on his own account; and all he asked of any free-trader was an occasional bribe to keep his eyes shut. Let him but receive notice (along with a gift of money) of any intended landing, and this jovial captain, with his grog-blossom nose and his husky voice, would take himself and his cutter off to another part of the coast until the landing was safely accomplished. What with the bribes and his own illicit traffic, he made a goodly pile; and by the time he was

dismissed the service (being found with his mate dead drunk one day on smuggled brandy), he was a rich man.

But then came this new broom, Captain Hawkhurst, a sharp, beaky-nosed, religious man, a teetotaller and a non-smoker, all hot to do his duty; and things became, as Zach said, 'tightened up' with a vengeance.

Of course, Captain Hawkhurst knew, as everybody knew, that the Jewels were smugglers. But the problem was to catch them at work. To this problem Captain Hawkhurst now devoted his energies, and it became a battle of wits between Hawkhurst on the one hand, and Zach and his allies on the other. But the whole county was behind Zach; and behind Captain Hawkhurst and his little cutter was nothing but the law of the land, which, in our isolated end of the country, we recognized only when we chose.

I have already told how on one of the *Mayfly*'s trips, Zach, being pursued by Hawkhurst, had been obliged

to sink his tubs and change gear with a crabber. Well, the next morning Captain Hawkhurst went 'creeping' for those tubs; that is, groping along the sea bottom with hooks, in the place he suspected them to be. And he found them, too, and great I'm sure must have been his feeling of triumph! He had hauled them up, carried them off to the Customs House, and took out a summons against Zach. Much good it did him! For how, as the magistrate pointed out, could Hawkhurst prove that the tubs he grappled up were the very same tubs as those he accused Zach of sinking? Hawkhurst couldn't prove it. And the magistrate dismissed the case.

'Now he'll be like a raging lion agin us,' said Zach, laughing. 'Or maybe he'll try some slydom or other. But we'll be ready for him, see if we won't! Slydom agin slydom, boy. I like that caper!'

It was a piece of 'slydom' that Hawkhurst elected to try for the second round in this battle of wits.

Zach told me about it: one early evening when the *Little Peter*, having made more than ordinary speed, was hove to some little distance off Hey's Mouth, waiting for darkness to run into Jewel's Cove, she was hailed by a small sloop flying the Swedish flag.

'You do business?' says the captain of the sloop when he came alongside.

'Don't mind if I do,' says Zach.

'How much for half anker?' says the Swedish captain.

'Thirteen shillings,' says Zach.

'I give you twel-uf,' says the captain.

'Done,' says Zach.

And so, without more ado, ten half ankers of brandy are transferred from the *Little Peter* to the sloop.

'That'll be a hundred and twenty shillings,' says Zach.

'I fetch it,' says the Swedish captain.

And what does that sloop do, when the captain was once back aboard, but haul down the Swedish flag, run up the Blue Ensign, and make off; while an English voice hails over the widening gap of water: 'Zachariah Jewel, I make a formal seizure of these kegs in the name of the law!' For the Swedish captain was no other than Captain Hawkhurst's first mate.

'Oh, do you?' sings out Zach. 'We'll see about that!' And the *Little Peter*'s guns crashed out, and sent the sloop's mainsail and jib flying in tatters.

'And what happened after that, Zach?' I asked.

'Oh, after that, boy, us had a bit of fun. We up sails and overhauled that sloop, and some of us boarded her, and we got them men – there was but five of 'em – all of a huddle with their guns took from them. And we put the ankers back in the lugger and took the sloop in tow.'

'Where is she now?' I asked.

'Well now, I wouldn't rightly know,' says Zach. 'On the

rocks, some place or 'nother. Maybe on the Garows or maybe on the Moels. But them five men we put to cool their heels on a bit of an island – Enys Eglos, if I'm not mistaken – to wait there for the tide to ebb and leave 'em scramble ashore. And after that they had a long walk home, I shouldn't wonder.'

'Captain Hawkhurst'll be *mad*!' I said gleefully.

'I wouldn't say you're wrong,' says Zach. 'And our men was mad, and all. They was for treating that mate rough, but I says no. He was but doing what he was bid, poor fellow.'

'And what do you think Hawkhurst will do now?'

'Somewhat,' said Zach thoughtfully. 'A bit of stirrage, may be.'

The 'bit of stirrage' was not long in coming. How Hawkhurst got wind of Zach's runs was a mystery, but get wind of them he did; and one dark night, when we were all down in Jewel's Cove unloading the *Little Peter*, old Sarah Jewel, Zach's mother, came fluttering down the cliff path with her petticoats tied up to her knees, and her little thin legs hopping and leaping like a frightened bird's.

'Revenue cutter!' she panted. 'Coming round the point b'yond Garrick Sands – her lights on and all!'

'Six boys up the cliff with me,' says Zach, naming the six quickly. 'And the rest into the caves. Haste now! Nay, leave the gear where 'tis.'

All hastened to do as he bid them. I wasn't one of the six named, but I scrambled up the cliff with them, all the same, for I had to be where Zach was. By the time the cutter hove in sight round the Cove rocks, Zach had his three cannon run out on to the cliff edge and loaded. He immediately opened fire, and for a short while the cliffs resounded with the boom of the cannon and the answering fire from the cutter's guns; with Gracie Winkey's screeching curses, as she danced there in the night behind the cannon, adding to the din. But we could see the cutter, and the men on her couldn't see us; and maybe Gracie Winkey's curses helped us, too; at any rate, I'm sure Zach thought they did. The cutter's fire went wide, and after a while she was fairly beaten off. She turned tail and disappeared round the rocks in the direction of Garrick Sands.

'Not that we've seen the last of her,' said Zach.

Leaving Sarah to keep watch, and two of the *Little Peter*'s crew, together with old Zeb, to stand by the cannon, the rest of us came down the cliff, and the men came out of the caves, and we worked with a will, unloading the lugger and carrying the goods up into the tunnel. Some way up, inside the cliff, the tunnel widened out into a sizeable chamber. Before dawn we had all our goods safely stored in this chamber; and all that was left in the lugger was a small load of apple barrels which Zach was due to deliver at Priddymouth.

I stayed to breakfast with the Jewels. And we had not long finished when the Revenue cutter came round the rocks again, and anchored in the Cove. From behind Jewel's wall, where the cannon were once more standing, we watched Captain Hawkhurst disembark and step into the *Little Peter*: watched him stooping and peering and prying, and going down into the cabin and coming up again, and, of course, finding nothing but the apple barrels. So then up the cliff path he comes, with his sword clanking at his side, and the mate, with *his* sword clanking, following on behind.

'Now us'll get indoors and have a bite more breakfast,' says Zach.

That's what we were doing when Captain Hawkhurst

knocked at the door: mighty busy with our plates and mugs, we were, though it was but pretence, for we were all full.

Zach got up and flung the door wide.

'Oh, 'tis you, Cap'n,' says he. 'And come to apologize, I reckon, for practising your guns at midnight so near shore, and disturbing an honest fam'ly in their well-earned rest! What's things coming to, I'd like to know, when folk can't sleep quiet in their beds, but you must be smashing the cliffs to jowds, and scaring folk nigh out of their wits with your bowldacious clacker?'

'Aye,' shrilled old Zeb at the top of his voice, 'the missus and me did think the end of the world was come; and if we bain't in fits the both of us, 'tis small thanks to you. My old woman was trimbling so the bed shook under her, and screeching like Tregeagle!'

'I had the head of me under the blankets,' screamed Sarah. 'For, thinks I, 'tis either Judgement Day, or 'tis old Scritch himself, come in a clap of thunder and lightning to carry we off.'

'And Matthy here down on his knees,' shouted Job, 'putting up a prayer for the lot of us! But I did say, "Out with us, boys, and strike a blow for the old country! 'Tis an invasion from out foreign, that's what it is!"'

'So then,' bawled Harry, 'out we goes, and fires off a shot or two from the little old cannon –'

They were all shouting together now, and Job was banging with his fist on the table. The crockery rattled and the rafters echoed. Captain Hawkhurst couldn't get a word in. I felt almost sorry for him, though my ribs were aching with my efforts not to laugh. He left at last, threatening something indistinct about the Jewels hearing more of this. And when he had gone we all burst out laughing.

The 'hearing more of it' was a farce. For though the

case was solemnly tried before a judge and jury, Captain Hawkhurst could bring no evidence that the Jewels had been engaged in smuggling that night; and even the matter of who first opened fire was considered not proven.

12

Taken by Surprise

But Captain Hawkhurst had 'pledged his mind', as we say, to catch Zach out, and the oftener he was foiled, the more determined he became. Also Tidecombe, who had recovered from his broken leg, was again 'on the rampage'. Now the two of them, Hawkhurst and Tidecombe, were working hand in glove to bring Zach to book.

Between runs, Zach would now most often be away, arranging for the *Little Peter*'s outward-bound cargoes. He bought a good horse, a red roan, called Jerry, and would be riding over the county, both to east and west, to do business with merchants and big farmers; who, to a man, not only supplied him openly with exportable goods, but gave him, secretly, heavy orders for contraband.

And while Zach was so engaged about cargo for the *Little Peter*, his three brothers, Matthy, Job, and Harry, would, in propitious weather, be slipping over to Roscoff in the *Mayfly*, for they were all itching to be up and doing. Well, one night, these three had not long arrived back, and we had unloaded and got the goods to the top of the cliff. Perhaps, Zach not being with us, we were less orderly and cautious than we should have been, I don't know; but we got a nasty surprise. I was busy, I remember, slinging two sacks of tobacco over the back of a patient moke, and thinking of nothing but that Zach would be returning before morning, and that I was not going home until I had seen him, when suddenly a cry rang out, 'Stand in the King's name!' and a crowd of men rushed up out of the darkness on all sides of us.

In the whirl of confusion that followed I could hear Tidecombe's voice, and Hawkhurst's, sharply giving orders – a joint attack of land and sea forces! I leaped away from the moke and began to run, felt my arm grabbed by someone, twisted round and got my foot between that someone's two feet, felt him release his hold, heard him thud to the ground, and fled on. I was over the wall into the Jewels' yard, and out over the wall on the other side and down the cliff and crouched hidden under a rock, all in a flash, and without a thought, as it seemed to me. And there I squatted, listening to the shindy up above – shouts, stamping feet, the *yaw-eh-haw* of the galloping mokes, and now and then a shot or two. To my excited nerves it seemed to go on for hours; and then, suddenly, all fell quiet.

I came out from under the rock, and stretched myself, for my hiding-place had been very low and I felt cramped. I stood there, listening. Not a sound. The Excise men had evidently gone. But what of our men? I hoped, and believed, that most of them would have got away, knowing the lie of the land, as they did, so much better than the Excise men. But what of Parson Lanyon? I felt a bit troubled about the parson, for his tubby little body was not much adapted to running. Well, if he had been taken, no doubt he would have some tale handy: some tale that no one would believe, but which it would be difficult to disprove. He was infinitely resourceful. And to circumvent Hawkhurst would be like honey to his mouth.

Heartening myself with suchlike assurances, and keeping my ears pricked, I went warily up the cliff again. There was no moon, of course, but it is never pitch-dark on a fine night by the sea; the sky was clear and the stars gave a little light. I passed beyond the yard wall of Jewel's Place, and tiptoed across the deserted battle-ground: not a man, not a moke, not a sign of the contraband. Well, Hawkhurst would have made a seizure of the contraband and removed it. What *would* Zach say when he came back? This was the first time that such a calamity had befallen us; and (unreasonably, I expect) I couldn't help thinking that if Zach had been there it wouldn't have happened.

I was feeling downhearted, and shivering a bit with the shock of it all, as I turned away from the scene of disaster, and went cautiously in through Jewels' yard, and pushed open the kitchen door. There was no one in the kitchen, and the place was in darkness. But under the door at the back of the kitchen there was a faint shine of light. After pausing to think and listen for a moment, I crossed the kitchen, quietly turned the handle of this second door, and went through into a room that had once been a parlour, but which was now used by Sarah and Zeb as a bedroom.

I stood with my hand still on the open door and stared in sheer astonishment. On the bed lay old Sarah, propped up on pillows. She was wearing a huge white nightcap, tied with a tape under her chin, and a bunchy bedgown with a frill at the neck. Her sharp little eyes were turned up to the ceiling, and her mouth was drawn down in a grimace of pain. Under the closely curtained window Zeb was stooping to wring out a handkerchief in a bowl of water, and this, as I stood gaping, he carried round the back of the bed and laid, with great ceremony, on Sarah's forehead. And beside the bed, by a table where a candle stuck into a bottle was burning and guttering, sat Parson Lanyon. He had an open Bible in his hand, and he was reading to Sarah, in a very loud and clear voice, the story of the ram caught in a thicket. He took not the slightest notice of my coming in, though the draught from the open door all but blew the candle out. I shut the door quickly behind me. And still none of them looked my way.

'"And Abraham lifted up his eyes, and looked, and beheld behind him a ram caught in a thicket by his horns",' read Parson Lanyon.

At this point Sarah gave a loud groan. Parson Lanyon paused, stooped a little nearer the bed, and said soothingly, 'There, there, my good woman, is the pain no easier?'

Suddenly I had a fit of the giggles; whereat the parson shut the Bible and turned towards me, beaming.

'Oh, so it's only you! I thought it didn't sound quite like Hawkhurst. But one can't be too careful.'

Sarah flung the handkerchief off her forehead, and leaped out of bed. 'Be 'em all gone?' she asked.

'Yes,' I said. 'There's not a sign of anyone outside.'

'It was a near squeak for me, though,' said Parson Lanyon. 'I only just managed to get in here. A touching scene, eh, Dick? Devoted parson visiting his sick parishioner at midnight. Well, well, what's a long walk in the dark when duty calls?'

'Wisht!' said Zeb. 'There's a step in the yard!'

Sarah bounded back into bed, turned up her eyes, and groaned. The parson reopened the Bible and read at random:

'"And Jonah was in the belly of the fish three days and three nights ...",' he began loudly.

''Tis only Harry!' cried Zeb, as the door burst open.

'Now, that's a very interesting point,' says Parson Lanyon. 'Why do people persist in asserting that Jonah was swallowed by a whale? We are distinctly told he was swallowed by a *fish*. A whale is not a fish: it may have been a shark, or a sea serpent, or some other now happily extinct monster of the deep. But certainly it was not a whale ... Ah, Harry – so you got clear! And what of the others?'

'I know no more'n you,' said Harry. 'But the goods is seized.'

'So I understand,' said the parson. 'Ah well, better luck next time.'

'He'll have his case agin us now,' said Harry dolefully.

'Pooh!' said Parson Lanyon. 'You forget, my man, the law is merciful.'

'Any road, let's get out of here!' said Sarah. 'What you think of a poor sick woman, Harry?'

She was up again, and doing a grotesque dance over the sanded floor, the huge nightcap bobbing on her little head and her tiny body looking quite shapeless in the bunchy bedgown. By and by she untied the nightcap, threw it from her, and pulled the bedgown off over her head. I saw then what made it so bunchy – she had all her clothes on underneath.

'Us be safe to light a fire, and have a cup of warm now, I s'pose?' she said. 'Do you go out and fetch in a faggot to put under the brandis, Harry, for me tongue's fair clemmed, and I could do with a dish of tea.'

We soon had a fire going in the kitchen and the kettle hung over it. And, while we were waiting for the water to boil, the other men came clattering in, in twos and threes. They had every one escaped; but most were bruised and one or two were limping; and they all looked rather wild and dirty. Zeb brought out a barrel of rum from a concealed cupboard under the stairs, and there were drinks, and drinks again, for everybody: Sarah and the parson and I drinking tea – laced, in Sarah's and the parson's case, with a good measure of rum, and in my own case with a little. For, as the parson said, 'It keeps out the cold, Dick, and steadies the nerves.'

My head began to go round; the kitchen was hot and smelled of the fish that were drying on racks under the beams, and of the men's salty and tarry jackets, and of the earth on their boots and breeches. The smoke from their pipes hung heavy in the room, and made my eyes smart. Despite the rum, we were not a particularly happy party; the men were grumbling and swearing, threatening what they would do to Hawkhurst if only they could catch him unawares. And the more they drank the angrier they grew.

In the midst of all this, there came a clatter of hoofs out in the yard, and they all sprang to their feet, some whipping out their pistols and others knives. Old Zeb snatched down a blunderbuss that hung above the chimney and levelled it at the door.

'It's Zach, you fools!' I cried. For I recognized the sound of Jerry's hoofs.

The door flung wide. It *was* Zach. He took a quick look at the crowd in the kitchen and gave a none-too-pleased laugh.

'By Golles!' said he. 'Here's a pretty crum-a-grackle! And how did it all come about, I should like to know? The mokes running wild, and their girths trailing – aye, I met a dozen of 'em – and you all in here with murder in your eyes, but nothing to show for it! And the moor out there jowded up like all the devils in hell had been dancing on it! And the goods – what's come to the goods?'

The men put away their weapons in a hurry and began to explain. All were loud in their wrath. They swore there must be a tongue-tabbas [informer] about. Now they would find out who he was, slit his throat from ear to ear, and drop his carcass into a deep pit among the mine-workings, where it would never more be seen. Aye, this they would do, and more! For what had he brought them to? Transportation or hanging – that would be the end of this night's work!

'Now see here,' said Zach, 'by what I can make of it, there's too much talk and too little doing. We'll leave that tongue-tabbas – if so there be one – till by and by. There's more important work on hand than threating he, I'm thinking.'

More important? How could anything be more important?

'Where's your wits?' says Zach. 'Them tubs. 'Tis a

special order. They be all promised, some to Lord Trembath, and some to Farmer Trevillian, and some to the Tinners' Arms up Pargannian way. I've never let none of our clients down yet. And I don't intend to begin. We must have them tubs back for my credit's sake. Aye, and we *will* have 'em back. They be our property, not Hawkhurst's.'

'That's right enough!' ''Tis God's truth!' 'There's no denying of it!' they all chorused.

'So cheer up, boys,' says Zach. 'What say? How about tomorrow night?'

It was astonishing how swiftly the men recovered their spirits. The idea of outwitting Hawkhurst after all had them all grinning and chuckling. And then and there, with Zach as adviser-in-chief, we joyfully laid our plans for an attack on the Customs House at Priddymouth for the following night.

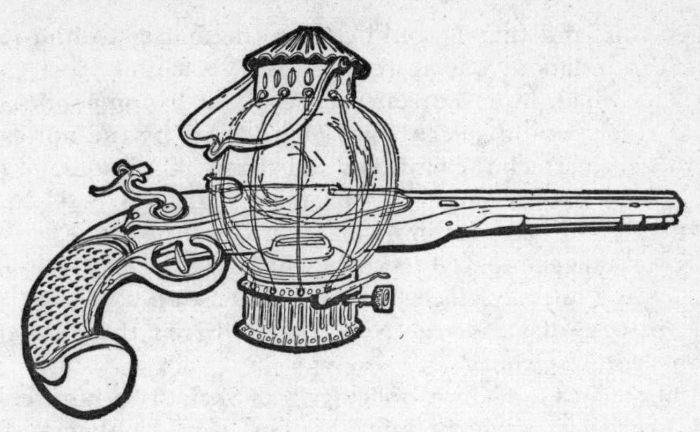

13

We Plan to Attack the Customs

For the attack on the Customs House the first need was horses, for the Jewels had none but Jerry. Parson Lanyon, who regretfully admitted that he must be left out of this venture, being on the wrong side of fifty, promised three. And I recklessly promised five, besides my cob, Diamond, whom I proposed to ride myself. Zach looked doubtful, and I had a horrid fear that he was about to suggest that I stayed behind with Parson Lanyon. However, after looking at me in a considering sort of way for a moment, he said:

'Well, you're a strapping lad, and a brave clever rider, and the cob is a good un, too. But what about Squire? I'm not going agin he, mind you, hosses or no.'

I assured him that my father would be entirely with us

over this, and that I would convey the matter to him in such roundabout way as would satisfy his whimsy.

That made nine horses. Zach thought a dozen horses and riders would suffice. Two men to stay by the horses, and ten to attack the Customs and remove the goods.

'There is but Willie Hosken there by nights,' said he. 'And I've a little plan in my head to keep *him* busy.'

Everyone clamoured to know what the plan was.

'Wait a bit,' says Zach. 'Hosses first. Fast ones they must be, in case of accidents. Now, boys, where's them other three coming from?'

There was not much difficulty. Les Skewish, a farm lad of Trevillian's, said he knew his boss would oblige with his bay hunter; and Digory Whear, a man who worked for Trembath, said he'd speak to his lordship and bring along two – one for himself and one for Matthy Jewel. They were eager in their promises, for to provide a horse meant, of course, to ride it, and no one wanted to be left out of this venture.

'So it's us four Jewels,' said Zach, 'and Dick here, and Les, and Digory. That makes seven men. Best way cast lots for t'other five. Parson here shall be the one to draw, and then we'll know 'tis all fair and fitty.'

So Sarah fetched a great iron saucepan and set it on the table, and each man dropped his pipe into it. Then the parson, with his eyes tightly screwed up, thrust his hand into the saucepan and drew out five pipes, one after the other. There were shouts of triumph as the five lucky men claimed their own and bitter oaths from the luckless ones.

'But you'm all be wanted,' explained Zach. 'There's the mokes, don't forget, to be kept hid in readiness, and brought out on a whistle, and I wouldn't say but that isn't the most important job of all.'

The men didn't think so; but, though they grumbled a bit, each one agreed to his allotted task. For Zach had them well disciplined, which was one reason for the astonishing success of his ventures.

'And now,' said Zach, 'about Willie Hosken, what keeps guard of a night-time. I'm thinking my Janey can help us over he. He fancies himself, does Willie; he's a rare one for the maidens, and he's something of a nog-head, though his mammy don't think so. Aye, I'll ride over come daylight and have a word with Janey. She's a bowerly maid enough to take a man's fancy.'

'Pretty as a pink,' we all agreed.

'Anyways,' said Zach, looking pleased, 'she can go to market in Priddymouth, I shouldn't wonder. And she can meet up with Willie, casual like –'

'She'll do more for 'ee than that, Zach,' said Digory. 'Any maid would.'

'That's as may be,' said Zach. 'But I'd have you remember that Janey ain't *any* maid – she's special.'

'Oh in course,' agreed Digory hastily.

'So Janey meets up with Willie Hosken casual like,' repeated Zach, 'and after a bit of flighty talk, she drops him a hint that she's minded to take a bit of a walk along the cliffs, or through the woods, come sundown. And then,' Zach laughed, 'I shouldn't wonder if Willie wouldn't be minded to take a bit of a walk along the cliffs, or through the woods, himself. And if Janey don't succeed in keeping him out long 'nough for us to do our job – well, she's not the maid I take her for.'

'I hope, though,' said Parson Lanyon anxiously, 'this Willie What's-his-name is not a rough fellow?'

'Nay,' said Zach. 'I told you – he's a nog-head. I've no fears for Janey – she'll wheedle him.'

'And if she don't succeed,' said Matthy, 'us can

always give un a scat on the noddle and tie un up, poor fellow.'

And then, all things being arranged to our satisfaction, we bid each other good night, and every man went to his home.

I had promised Zach to speak to my father, and so, finding him in a good though somewhat dreamy mood at breakfast, I said lightly:

'I think, sir, there'll be five of our horses taking a gallop tonight.'

'Will there indeed?' said my father.

'It's a kind of a – race, to Priddymouth and back,' I explained. 'I myself shall be riding Diamond.'

'I see,' said my father gravely. 'And what occasions this – race, if I may venture to inquire?'

'Zach's cargo has been taken by thieves.'

'How extremely reprehensible!' said my father.

'So we propose to get it back.'

'Well, naturally,' agreed my father, 'Zach must endeavour to retrieve what belongs to him – if he can?'

'Oh yes, he can,' I assured him. 'It's all planned out.'

'I'm glad to hear that,' said my father, 'But, Dick –'

'Yes, sir?'

'Watch Diamond's steps in the dark. If you have a fall, and – er – if someone should have to pick you up, I shall be more than annoyed.'

'Zach says I shan't have a fall – none of us will.'

'Very good,' said my father. 'I ask no more.'

And no more was said.

With Nathaniel, our steward, I could be more open. Indeed, I told him everything, and it was he who advised me which horses to take, as being the most steady and dependable, and helped me to bring them in, and brought me a pile of thick woollen stockings to muffle their feet with. He insisted on saddling them himself, too, paying particular attention to the saddle girths.

'You may have a hot gallop,' he said, 'and it wouldn't do for a girth to snap or go slack. Have 'em looked to again, Dick, afore you set off for home.'

I promised him I would. But I was so excited and impatient, I scarce knew what I was saying. Nathaniel shook his head.

'If you can't keep cool, best way stop home,' he warned me.

'I *am* cool!' I burst out. 'I was never cooler in my life!'

'Well, well,' said Nathaniel. 'Only I'd have you remember that in a job like this the lives of all be in the hands of each. 'Tis much, boy, that Zach'll take 'ee.'

'Yes, I know,' I answered, somewhat sobered. 'I won't let Zach down, Nathaniel, indeed I won't!'

As soon as it was dark, Nathaniel and I set off for the rendezvous, each riding a horse and leading two. I had my gun slung over my shoulder, and it made me feel very manly. Though how I should feel if it came to a shooting fray, I didn't know, having in all my life, so far, shot nothing larger than a rabbit. The rendezvous was a wooded dip behind the cliffs to the east side of our hamlet, and there the eleven other riders and the six other horses were soon assembled.

It was going to be a stiff ride, and one it would be impossible to hasten, for we were not venturing to use the bridle paths, much less the turnpike road, lest we fall foul of Tidecombe; but were to keep mainly to the cliffs and the wild moor behind them. We had, too, to strike well inland at one point to ford the Venton river, secretly making its way among tangled woods and a maze of creeks down to the sea. But we had plenty of time, not proposing to get to the Customs House before one in the morning.

The men with the donkeys had set out long before. All through the day the donkeys had been arriving in Priddymouth, on one pretext or another: some with fish to sell, others with vegetables; this one to be shod, that one to be fitted with a new bridle. Now, well greased, and with muffled hoofs, they would be waiting for us in a net store, belonging to one Spargo, a crony of Zach's, on the wharf hard by the Customs House. We had no fear of any of the townsfolk; we were sure of their sympathy. And, if Janey had played her part well, we should have no fear of Willie Hosken. It was the watchfulness of Hawkhurst that we had to guard against. But Zach had chosen his time cunningly. The tide would be well out, and, the Customs House standing on a bay of the slow-flowing Priddy river, it would not be possible for the cutter to make a landing, because of mudbanks. The only mischance would be should Hawkhurst happen not to be on board the cutter, but in the town somewhere. We had to risk that.

Having seen us all mounted, Nathaniel bid us Godspeed, and took himself off in the darkness to walk back to the manor. And we set out at a sober trot, Zach leading, and I keeping as close to his side as might be.

It was a silent ride, for we were much occupied in watching our horses' steps among the rocks and thorn bushes, and the bogs and abrupt dips and rises of that wild country. The scarce audible *pud-a-pud-pud* of the muffled hoofs, the sudden stumbling of a horse, and the whispered oath of its rider, the subdued roar of the sea on our right hand, the sigh of the wind among the thorns, the churr of a nightjar flattened against a boulder, and the swift beating wings of some awakened bird – these were the sounds that accompanied us. And all this commingling of stealthy-seeming sounds, bound up as it was with the high thrill of the adventure we were on, kept my mind at such a fine stretch that I could have laughed aloud (had laughter been permitted) from sheer crazy intoxication.

And then, of a sudden, I found myself flying over Diamond's head and I landed in a bog, which Diamond had heeded and jibbed at, and which I, in my exhilaration, had ignored.

I scrambled up, muddy from head to foot, and much mortified. Dim against the cloudy night I saw the shapes of the other riders moving ahead of me. Nobody had taken the least notice of my fall, and I understood that it was up to me to go more warily, or to be left to make my unhappy way home again.

I felt terribly ashamed. I would rather Zach had turned and cursed me. To be ignored, as of no consequence, was almost more than I could bear. I longed for a chance to show Zach what mettle I was made of, and vowed to myself that I would do something, however rash, to prove my worth before the night was out. But for the moment there was nothing to do but to keep my chagrin to myself, watch every inch of the ground, subdue every rhapsodical imagining, and move on after the others.

Pud-a-pud-pud, pud-a-pud-pud: the low sound of the muffled hoofs, and the rumour of the sea, and the stir of the wind – it went on and on and on. We were going downhill now, into the valley of the Venton river: first down a slope of bracken, and then into the deep darkness of the woods. And now, from beyond the woods, came the faint chuckle of the outflowing tide, as the water flirted against the river-bank, or wavered round some fallen branch or bar of sand.

Under low-stooping trees on the verge of the river, Zach pulled up, and we all gathered round him.

'I'm for swimming across,' says he, 'the river's running sweet and suant here, and 'twill save us a good five mile.

But if any of you ain't sure of your hosses, we'll have to make up-river to the ford.'

We were all sure of our horses, we told him.

'Right then,' says Zach. 'Here's for it.'

And down a bit of a bank we rode and into the shallows, and on from the shallows into deeper water, feeling the river run swift against our thighs, and so across into the shallows again, and out on to a gravelly beach, where the horses stood for a moment to shake the water from their streaming sides.

Here Zach gave us our final orders.

'Soon as we reach the moor above Priddymouth,' says he, 'we take the lane that comes down by the back of Customs Wharf. Near the bottom of the lane there's a withy copse on the left, and 'tis there we'll leave the hosses. Les and Digory will stay with 'em, but not fasten 'em up without they be over-restive, for we may want 'em quick.'

Les and Digory! I thanked my stars! I had feared for a moment that to stay by the horses would be my unheroic lot. And then came the humiliating thought that perhaps, after my disgraceful fall, Zach was not going to trust me even with this job ... Oh, but I would show him – if only I got the chance!

'The rest of us will get down to the back of the Customs House,' went on Zach. 'And there, under the shadow of the wall, every man will wait, while I nip along to Spargo's store, pick up the tools he'll have left lying handy, go from there to the front of the Customs House and get busy on the lock of the door. No man will stir till he hears my signal – 'twill be an owl wickering – and then you'll all come round, quick and quiet as you can, to join me. But if aught goes amiss, you'll either hear me holler, and that'll mean there's to be a fight for it, and you'll come round smart with your guns ready; or you'll hear me fire one shot, and that'll mean all's up and it's each man to get away best he can.'

'It won't come to that,' said Job grimly.

'I should say it won't,' agreed Zach. 'But us has to be ready for aught that may come. Now, if all's clear –'

'It ain't,' said Harry. 'Who's keeping the look-out?'

'The men waiting with the mokes in Spargo's store,' said Zach. 'Soon as I pick up the tools, there'll be four of 'em come out, one to watch at each corner of the Customs House. *Their* signal, if they see aught, will be a fox barking. Right? Then we'll get on our way, and steady all!'

14
The Attack

Between Venton river and Priddymouth we were able to get down on to a wide bay under the cliffs, and on hard sand we went at a gallop and made good speed. I should say it was not much past midnight when we came off the sand and up a steep rise on to Priddymouth Moor. From here we could see the vague jumble of the town ahead of and below us, and the riding light of the Excise cutter shining well out beyond the river-mouth.

Taking a circuit above the town, where everyone, it seemed, was a-bed, for not a light showed, we came to a lane that descended sharply to the river-bank. Near the bottom of this lane, by the withy copse Zach had spoken of, we dismounted, led the horses in under the trees, and left them to the care of Les and Digory. The rest of us, at a quick run, went on down the lane, till we came to the flat dim expanse of Customs Wharf, and saw the long low line of Spargo's store and the tall square bulk of the Customs House blotched against a faint gleam of river-water and mud-bank.

At the corner of Spargo's store a light shone for a moment, and was instantly quenched: the signal that the men with the donkeys were safely housed within and on the look-out for us. With a wildly beating heart I watched Zach slip like a black ghost over to the store. The rest of us took our stand under the windowless back wall of the Customs House, and there we waited for what seemed like an eternity. I felt it terrible to have to stand there doing nothing, and the great hazard of what we were at – the risk of discovery, the possibility of a fight, or, worse, the sudden need for flight – came upon me all in a clap for the first time that night. I stood with my back pressed against the wall, and set my teeth. If I couldn't do anything else for Zach, I could at least die for him: no Hawkhurst should take him except over my dead body, I told myself.

And then – *to-wic, to-wic, to-wic*! Such a little sound in the silence of the night, but it seemed to run right through me with a sharp quiver from head to foot and had every nerve in my body tingling. Now I was racing with the rest to the front of the Customs House, where the door swung wide; and now we were all through the door, and Zach had closed it noiselessly behind us. And we stood in a darkness black and musty as the inside of a bag.

'All safe,' whispered Zach. 'No one here. Janey's done *her* part, it seems.'

He lit a small lantern he was carrying, but that only made the surrounding blackness seem more profound; for the lantern itself was blackened on three sides and on three parts of the fourth side, leaving but a tiny circle through which the light could shine. With this little light, Zach went clambering and peering among the piles of goods ranged about the great stone floor; and, as he moved, the rounded sides of barrels, the rough bulge of sacks, and the square ends of wooden chests gleamed in the light for an instant, and vanished again. At last, from a corner under the barred windows, I heard his low voice.

'Here be our goods, the lot of 'em, stacked up together. Now, boys, everyone take your load, and quick and quiet.'

It was not easy work in the dark, with only the little gleam of Zach's lantern to guide us inside, and an even smaller glimmer showing through the once more open door, where the men with the donkeys were now all waiting. The piles of goods stacked about the floor seemed to have taken on a tantalizing life of their own, and to be continually shifting their positions and rising up in unexpected places to bar one's progress. I found myself bumping into barrels, barking my shins against the sharp edges of wooden boxes, and, ever and anon, colliding with another human body that was making for the door with the same urgency as myself. But with all this seeming confusion we were nevertheless getting out the goods at a rare speed; and as each donkey was loaded it was led away into the night, to take such secret and solitary way to Trevy

Downs as its owner deemed best. Soon all were gone, and there remained but a few tubs which we were to take with us up to the copse and carry before us on the horses. Everything had gone so smoothly that now my previous thoughts of the hazards we were running seemed but airy foolishness.

We had the remaining tubs outside, and Zach, with a chuckle, was drawing the Customs House door shut behind us, when there came the sound of running steps from the direction of the town.

Every man's hand went to his gun, and immediately dropped again. For it was Janey.

'Willie Hosken!' she gasped. 'I had him nicely foxed out there on the cliff, till – till all to once he come to his sense of duty. I fetched him a clout over the ear, but it wasn't forceful enough to do more than stagger him. "It's a plot!" says he, and sets off running to the town –'

'Well,' said Zach, 'he is but one.'

'Nay,' says Janey, all but crying. 'Cap'n Hawkhurst's lodged in the town this night – he and all his men – and Willie stopped to wake him – that's how I got the start of him. Oh, get away, get away quick! They'll all be on you in the space of ten minutes!'

'Time enough,' says Zach. 'Now, boys, shoulder them tubs and up the lane and off. And you, my maid, shall ride before me on Jerry.'

We all took our tubs, and made what speed we could with the weight of them up the lane. I was carrying the lantern, which Zach had passed over to me, so that he could give a hand to Janey. Glancing back in the direction of the town, we could see a light wavering up among the houses from a hidden street, and one or two windows lit up as well.

'Aye,' said Zach, 'they're gathering. But it'll take 'em a

good few minutes. They won't risk coming without a number.'

'Oh, Zach,' cried Janey, 'I'm sorely vexed to have failed you!'

'Nay, never say that,' answered Zach. 'You've done bravely well. Show us a glim, boy Dick, to heave up the tubs by.'

We had reached the copse now, and were bringing out the horses. Under the heavy gloom of the trees, I moved the lantern now here, now there, as the men heaved up their burdens and sprang into the saddles. The little circle of light fell on Matthy, who had his foot in a stirrup and was clutching a large sack to his chest.

'What's this?' exclaimed Zach. 'What you got there? That sack ain't ours! *That* never came off the *Mayfly*!'

'What if it didn't?' says Matthy defiantly. ''Tis ours now. Us can do with an extra bit of baccy to reward us for this night's work.'

'Make me out a thief, you bastard, would you?' says Zach grimly. 'We're taking none but our own.'

'Nay, but Zach –'

'Take it and put it back,' says Zach.

Put it back! What madness! More lights were showing from the town. The men's nerves were all wrought up. They began to protest strenuously.

'I'm not stirring till Matthy goes back with that sack,' said Zach.

'I wain't!' says Matthy, scrambling on to his horse. ''Tis as much as my life is worth! Do you want me to swing?'

Then it came upon me, like a great burst of light, that here was the chance I had been waiting for – to redeem myself in Zach's eyes for that blundering fall.

'Give it to me,' I cried. '*I'll* take it back!'

'Keep off!' cried Matthy.

But I caught his horse by the bridle with one hand, and the sack with the other, and, while the animal reared and plunged, I dragged the sack to the ground, picked it up, leaped with it on to Diamond's back and galloped off down the lane.

'Don't wait for me,' I called over my shoulder. 'I shan't come back this way!'

I heard them making off up the lane. I heard too, more ominously, the jingling of a company of horse and riders, coming along the flat that led from the town to Customs Wharf. But I reached the Customs House, and was off Diamond and in through the door, and had the sack dropped inside, almost before I had time to think. And then I stood for a moment, with my heart drumming against my ribs.

The beat of hoofs was drawing nearer and nearer, and I could distinctly hear Captain Hawkhurst's voice shouting out some order. What could I do to give our men a chance to get clear away? To get clear away myself? Though my getting away didn't seem to matter so much: it was Zach they would be after, it was Zach they would hang! I had taken the lantern from under my coat to guide me through the door, and now, by its light, I saw a long coil of rope at my feet. I snatched it up and hurried out with it, for now I had an idea. One end of the rope I fastened to an iron bar of the window on the right-hand side of the door, with the other end I ran diagonally across the wharf to where an old tree leaned out across the track that led to the town. Looping the end of the rope to a branch at about breast height, I pulled the rope taut and made it fast. That would delay them! The horses could not pass under it; and it was not likely they would leap over it in the dark – not, at least, till someone had dismounted and scanned it, lest some other obstacle lay behind. At any rate, it was the best I could do. But it was a near go for me. I had but just got to the Customs House door and on to Diamond's back when the foremost of the Excise men came clear of the town track and on to the wharf.

I heard the skitter of the horse's hoofs, as it came up against the rope and stopped dead. I heard the man shout. But you may be sure I didn't stay to see what they made of my trap! I was away on the instant; not up the lane, for then, if they followed me, I should be leading them direct on the track of Zach and the rest. No, I plunged in among the thick woods by the river-bank, along a bridle path that should bring me eventually to Venton.

I had ridden that path a score of times, but now, in the blackness of the woods, and with only the dull gleam of the river here and there to guide me, I lost myself repeatedly. At one point, finding myself off the track, and in a tangled glade that seemed to lead nowhere, I pulled up to listen. But I heard nothing save a little whispering from the leaves over my head. So I came slowly down the glade again, struck the bridle path once more, and galloped on. And still nothing broke the silence but the soft sound of Diamond's muffled hoofs on the grassy track.

Could they not be following me, after all? Could something, the impress of horses' feet in the shine of a searching lantern, perhaps, have led them not through the woods after me, but up the lane after the others? At the thought, I pulled up and fired my gun into the air, and the reverberation of the shot in that silence seemed loud enough to bring a whole host of pursuers on my heels, and set me off galloping faster than ever.

The path had left the river-bank now and was heading more westerly, so that I had not even the occasional gleam of the river to guide me: only between the blackness of trees a faintly lighter streak where the path ran. But I knew that if I could but keep the track I should reach the high country above Venton. And, at last, yes, here were the woods giving back, and the path going uphill, and at the top of the hill I was on the wide, bleak, open flat of Venton Downs, with the town of Venton lying to the west of me.

Before venturing over the downs I reined up again, and listened. And now, through a stillness where nothing stirred, I could hear, though very faint, the far-off drum of galloping hoofs. I could see, too, little red flashes in the darkness behind me, and knew that Hawkhurst's men must be firing their pistols as they rode, to what purpose I could not guess. Then it came upon me, with horror, that perhaps some of our men had come off the moor, and were now on the same track as I was, and nearer to danger than myself.

I clapped my heels against Diamond's flanks, and we were off again, going faster than perhaps I had ever ridden in my life. And so into Venton, and plunging down the steep main street between the darkened houses, where a window opened here, and a light suddenly shone there, as we galloped by. I was making for the turnpike road. I dared not risk turning off on to the moors at the pace I was going, lest we come a fall and I break my neck, or Diamond his back.

'Watch Diamond's steps in the dark. If you have a fall, and – er – if someone should have to pick you up, I shall be more than annoyed.' I remembered my father's words, and knew what he meant by them: not a fall that would break my neck, but a fall that would bring us into trouble with the Excise. But there should be neither kind of fall, if Diamond and I knew it!

I was shouting now at the top of my voice, for just ahead of me was the turnpike gate, with its array of spiked bars that a horse might not venture to leap in the dark.

'Open, Nicky, open! It's Dick Pellew, your old friend, Dick Pellew! Open and let me through, Nicky; my life's in your hands! Open, open, Nicky!'

It seemed an age, though it was, I suppose, but a few moments before the toll-house door opened and old Nicky Trivet, carrying a huge lantern, shuffled out, bare-foot and coughing. He was in his bedgown, and his little, sleep-dimmed eyes blinked up in astonishment at me from under his nightcap. But he swung the gate wide without question.

'The Excise men are after me,' I shouted. 'Hold them – be asleep in your bed and wake but slowly. Take your time with the gate. And – I haven't passed this way, Nicky, you can stake your life on it, I haven't!'

'Nay, nay,' answered the old man with a grin. 'You ain't passed this way, boy. Not a body's passed this way since I went to my bed these hours agone!'

'But, Nicky, you must keep awake! You must watch! And should any of our boys be behind me, let them through with all your speed!'

'Aye, aye,' said Nicky. 'I'll let 'em through.'

'I'll remember it,' I cried, as I urged Diamond to a gallop again. 'There'll be some baccy for you soon – and rum!'

And along the turnpike we galloped, Diamond and I, and didn't slacken pace till we turned off into the familiar ways at the back of Pellew Manor. And there I slowed Diamond into a walk. Now every foot of the ground was familiar to me, and I could take such turns as defied pursuit, and I knew at last that we were safe.

When I reached home I found Nathaniel waiting up

for me. The good fellow was in the stableyard with a light almost as soon as I got there.

'My lor,' says he, as I slid all in a stagger off Diamond's back, 'the cob's in some shape! I wouldn't say but you've had a hard ride of it. Here, leave him to me, I'll see to a bran mash for him. And you're in some shape yourself! Get you indoors – there's meat and drink for you ready in the kitchen.'

'I'm not in any shape at all!' I answered indignantly. Though, indeed, I was quite lightheaded, and the ground seemed to be floating past me, as if I were still galloping over it, as I made my way into the kitchen.

It was some half-hour or more before Nathaniel joined me. Meanwhile I had been striding aimlessly up and down, with now and then an exclamation, and now and then a laugh; for though there was a meal laid out for me on the kitchen table, I was in no mood to eat.

'You brought it off, then, I take it?' said Nathaniel.

'Yes, Nat, we brought it off,' I answered. 'We brought –'

And all at once I broke into loud, hysterical laughter, which Nathaniel reduced to giggling and gasping protests by seizing up a pailful of cold water and pitching it over my head.

15
Kappen's Warning

Looking back next day on my night's adventure, I was at one moment convinced that I had run a terrible risk and the next moment telling myself that I had run no risk at all. But whether I had or hadn't, I was amply rewarded by Zach's words to me, though they were few enough.

'You did a brave job for me, Dick boy,' he said. And that was all. But I kept repeating those words to myself, and they filled me with pride. They filled me, too, I regret to admit, with a rare sense of my own importance; as if I, and I alone, had saved Zach from the gallows. Whereas all I had really done was to carry out an obstinate whim of his – a whim which might well have brought the whole night's work into jeopardy.

I told him about the flashes of firing I had seen, and asked if any of our men had been behind me. And he said, yes, three of them had struck off the moors and on to Venton Downs, as being easier going.

'But not by my counsel,' he said. 'I was all agin it. And if it hadn't been that Nicky Trivet was waiting at the gate to let 'em through, and if he hadn't held up Hawkhurst and the rest as was at their heels – and I reckon that was your doing, Dick? – well, then three would be in irons this morning.'

At which speech the pride in myself swelled prodigiously, though I affected indifference.

By the end of that day the raid on the Customs House was being talked of from one end of the county to the other. And, of course, though everyone feigned ignorance, there was not a soul but knew in his heart that Zach was at the bottom of it. And Captain Hawkhurst was in no doubt at all. 'A bird,' as Gracie Winkey would say, brought us tidings of his strange remark. 'It can be none other than Zach Jewel, for he is an honourable man, and has touched nothing that was not his.' Which seemed to us an admission that the Excise was in the wrong, and the smugglers in the right. But, mind you, Captain Hawkhurst could never have made that remark if Zach had not insisted on the return of the tobacco sack. And there again, I – but enough of me and my petty pride!

But, honourable as he admitted him to be, that night's work made Captain Hawkhurst all the more determined to put an end to Zach's activities, and that seemed to me peculiarly unjust of him. For the only way to put a stop to Zach's activities was to catch him red-handed; and, once caught, Zach could expect no mercy, even though all the county stood solid behind him. For Hawkhurst would see to it that he was not tried by a local jury. And what a topsy-turvy state of mind must be Hawkhurst's, to wish to hang an 'honourable man'! A devotion to duty gone completely crazy and inhuman, so it seemed to me.

However, for the time Zach was safe. It was no use Hawkhurst's claiming to have seized contraband goods from the *Mayfly*, since he could not produce them. Nor was there any evidence to prove who it was that had broken into the Customs House. We were a bit anxious lest Janey should get into trouble; but Willie Hosken swore he had no idea what girl it was – and if he had any idea, all the more credit to him! The poor fellow fell into deep disgrace, and was dismissed the service for his part in the night's doings. Janey took this much to heart; but, as Zach said, a Cornishman who goes and ties himself up with such poor trash as the Excise has only himself to thank if he comes a fall.

'I would offer him a share in the *Little Peter* to make up, if I could,' Zach assured Janey. 'But what can I do? He ain't reliable.'

It was a relief to us all when we heard that Willie, turning his steps disconsolately away from home and making up-country, had been pressed on his way through Bristol, and was now earning his keep in the King's navy.

'He'll do well enough out on the sea away from the maidens,' said Zach to me. 'I wouldn't say but what he'll make a pretty sailor when the fantades is knocked out of him. And if Janey's taught him a sharp lesson, it was what he was in need of. But what troubles me, Dick, is not this Willie, but the talk of that there tongue-tabbas the boys are all on about. For though I make light of it to them, it sticks in my mind that someone must have given Hawkhurst word the other night when the *Mayfly* was unloading.'

'But who on earth could it be?' I asked.

'Dunno,' said Zach. 'That Dutchy boy of yours – couldn't be he, I s'pose?'

'Neil? But he can't speak, Zach!'

'I'll own he *don't* speak,' said Zach. 'But that's not to say he can't. It's a rum go about that Dutchy. Don't know what to make of him. No harm, anyways, in keeping your eye on him.'

I assured Zach I would. I didn't know what to make of Neil myself. I had defended him to Kappen, because whatever Kappen said seemed to rouse opposition in me. But Zach's suspicions were quite another matter. I began to pay the lad much more attention. I returned to my neglected task of teaching him to write, in which task good Parson Lanyon encouraged me; though from motives, I'm sure, now very different from my own. For my motive was nothing more than to keep him in my company, and to try to get to the bottom of what he was and thought. For this reason I would steal upon him when he was at work about the place; and, even at night, I would sometimes creep up to the garret where he slept, and listen at the door; as if to assure myself that he really was in bed, and hadn't slipped out of the window and made off on some secret spying expedition that would bring Zach into trouble.

One night, as I was listening at his door, it came over me how foolish I was; for whether he was inside or not, how could I tell by standing there? And with that thought, I turned the handle noiselessly and slipped into his room.

And there he was in bed and asleep, lying on his back, with a glint of moonlight shining on his round, pale face.

I stood for a moment looking at him, ashamed now of

my suspicion. And, as I so stood, he stirred and sat up – and uttered such a scream of terror that my heart almost stopped beating. He jerked up his arm in front of his face, and rocked himself from side to side, still screaming. I was so terrified myself that for a moment I couldn't move or speak; and what terrified me perhaps more than all was that in the screaming I seemed to distinguish words. But if they *were* words, they were not English, nor intelligible to me.

I had become so used to his complete silence that I was as much taken aback as if the door itself had suddenly found a voice and screamed out words at me. It was not till he lay down again, moaning and sobbing, and with his arm still across his face, that I was able to speak myself.

'It's only me, Neil,' I said. 'What are you frightened of? I came just to – just to – to see if you were all right.'

I don't know if he heard me, or if he understood. He buried his face in the pillow, and made that gesture with his hand as if he were trying to push something horrid away from him. And he was still drawing his breath in frightened sobs. I tried to speak kindly to him. I tried to pull the pillow from his face! but he clung to it with both hands, still sobbing; so I could do nothing but go out of the room again, feeling I had made a rare mess of whatever it was I had been trying to do, and not at all sure of exactly what I *had* been trying to do.

Next morning, when I approached him – he was grooming my father's stallion, Wallace, at the time – he flung down the curry comb and rushed out of the stable and hid somewhere. I didn't get a sight of him again for the whole of that day.

I finished grooming Wallace myself, and then I went to my father.

'How long are we going to keep Neil, sir?' I asked.

'How long, Dick?' said he. 'As long as he behaves himself, to be sure. Why do you ask?'

'I – don't quite know. I can't make him out, that's all.'

'Is there any reason why you should make him out?' asked my father.

'No. I suppose not. Only –'

'If a lost dog comes to my door,' went on my father, 'I take it in. I give it food and shelter. It may be an attractive animal, it may be a cowed and frightened one; but for that its previous owner must be held responsible. For my part, as long as it doesn't bite me, I treat it humanely. If it *does* bite me, then, naturally, it is time to reconsider. But I think, Dick – I may be wrong, of course – but I think' (my father gave his flickering smile) 'that Neil has not bitten anyone as yet?'

I left him, feeling irritated. I took it hard that my father should put up this barrier between himself and me. Why couldn't I tell him straight out what Zach had said to me and what my trouble was? I was in no mood for the elaborate hints and circumlocutions he delighted in. Truly I felt he was putting an unfair burden on me: and it was a relief to leave him and go to my lessons with the more simple-minded parson.

I found the parson still sitting over breakfast.

'Why, Dick,' said he, 'you're early, aren't you? Or is it that I'm late? But you're looking uncommonly serious! What's the news this morning?'

'Nothing much, sir,' said I. 'Only I'm sure that Neil can speak if he wants to.'

'That's good news indeed!' said Parson Lanyon, beaming at me. 'And what makes you think so?'

I told him how I had been up to the garret, though I didn't tell him why, because I was afraid he would rebuke me for thinking evil, where no evil was. (I don't believe the parson could think ill of anyone, except for a moment, in a fit of exasperation, as when he had called Doctor Treglown an ass.) I merely said that I had wanted to see if Neil was comfortably asleep, and how he had waked in a fright, and in his fright had spoken – yes, I was sure of it.

Parson Lanyon was delighted, though he read me a little homily on my lack of sensitivity. 'You went the wrong way to work, my boy,' said he. 'That poor lad has doubtless been through some terrible experience in his young life. Most like he woke from a nightmare in which some dreadful scene was being re-enacted. However, clumsy as you were, if he has found his voice, no doubt good will come of it. You must be patient and tender with him, Dick; let him feel he has a true friend in you. And then maybe – who knows? – in God's good time he may open his heart to you. He understands what you say to him, doesn't he?'

'Yes,' I said. 'I'm sure he understands English perfectly. And he can write quite a lot of English words.'

'That's the way, Dick! Keep it up! Give him all the spare time you have. We are told not to be weary in well-doing. And that reminds me – you and I, we mustn't neglect our tasks, either. No, I won't have any more breakfast. I'm rotund enough already. As old Langland says, "All is not good for the ghost that the guts asketh." "Ghost", in this context, signifying not an apparition in a white sheet, but the soul. It would be better for me if I could remember that saying more often. The truth is, Dick,' said he, feeling his paunch ruefully, 'I'm something of a glutton, God forgive me! And gluttony, we are told, is one of the seven deadly sins. Ring the bell, there's a good fellow, and we'll have temptation removed for the time being.'

The table was cleared and I opened my books. But the thoughts of both of us were straying. Mine to Neil, and how best to keep an eye on him, and how to be 'patient and tender' when I didn't particularly feel like being either: the parson's to the recent raid on the Customs House, an adventure which so delighted him that he must hear every detail of it again and yet again.

I did try my best to encourage Neil; and, whatever it was that had frightened him that night, it seemed that his confidence in me soon returned. It seemed that he wanted to please me, and it was quite touching to watch the efforts he took with his writing. One day he came to my room with his copy-book, and showed me a page, empty except for one word which he had written very large in the middle of it. The word was 'Sorry'.

He looked from the word to me, and back to the word, and then slowly drew his forefinger along under the letters, as if he were trying to underline them.

'That's good writing, Neil,' I said. 'But sorry for what?'

He sat down at my table, took up a pencil, thought for a moment, and began to write slowly, holding his left arm and hand to shadow the page so that I could not see what he was writing. When he had finished and held out the page to me, he was gazing at me with an intent and troubled look.

This is what he had written:

'Not fritened of boy Dick. Boy Dick is good.'

I told him I was glad to know that. And then I took the pencil in my turn and corrected his spelling, smiling at him to show that I was pleased. Whereat his round, troubled face broke into a smile, too. He took my hand and held it for a moment. Then he dropped it, picked up the pencil and wrote 'frightened, frightened, frightened' three times, as I had taught him to do when he made an error.

'That's right, Neil,' I said.

I held out my hand for the pencil, thinking to teach him some more words; but he hadn't done with his writing yet. Again he covered what he next wrote with his arm and hand, and when he showed it to me, his face was kind of lit up as I had never before seen it.

'Boy Dick is Neil's good friend.'

I suppose we most of us go down before a touch of flattery. I know that from that moment I began to think more of Neil, and even told myself that surely Zach must have been mistaken in suspecting him.

Meanwhile, through that autumn and early winter, despite Hawkhurst's vigilance, the *Little Peter* made so many successful runs that everyone was in good heart. What with the legitimate cargoes and the cunningly concealed contraband, Zach told me he was making a little fortune, and saving it up to buy a farm for his old age. 'When me limbs is gone a bit stiff for this work,' he explained.

The crew, too, were making money at a fine rate – and spending it at a fine rate. 'Drinking theirselves silly,' as Roger Kappen said. But that I put down to envy. They were always sober enough when it came to handling the boat, and what they did betweenwhiles seemed to me to be none of Kappen's business. I still felt a dislike for the man, and didn't see more of him than I could help, though, of course, we were bound to meet from time to time.

One mild winter morning, when I was passing his place on my way to Tiger Ellick's with a pair of riding-boots to be mended, I saw him out in his little croft, turning the earth with tremendous energy. I would have ridden past without stopping, could I have so managed, but he hailed me, flung down his long-handled shovel, and came to stand at my side, laying one hand on Diamond's neck, as if to prevent me from moving away.

'So,' says he, 'everyone's making their fortunes, seems so, except poor old Roger. But mark my words, boy, I'm well out of it. There's going to be trouble in that quarter. Aye, it's plain to see as the nose on your face. Throwing money about like water, ain't they? And what comes of that? Trouble. That's what comes of it.'

I didn't know what to say, so I said nothing.

'I've got me eyes open, I have,' he went on. 'I think a mortal lot of that man Zach Jewel; I wouldn't like no harm to come to he. And often, night-times, I'm on the watch for his sake, when you might think I'd be more comferable sleeping in me bed. Now mark me, Dick, Cap'n Hawkhurst ain't being fooled; he's artful as a bag of monkeys, and he's but lying low and biding his time. I hears a whisper, now and again, of what he's got in mind. How do I come to hear them whispers? Now, never mind. I've got me ways of drawing folks out when I go to Priddymouth. And why do I go to Priddymouth?' (Here Kappen gave me a most hideous wink.) 'To sell me broccolo and a shot rabbit or two, to be sure. You best warn Zach. From what I do hear, Jewel's Cove ain't safe no more. You tell him from me to land some other place, and change that place frequent, or he'll be nabbed, boy, afore the winter's out. Now you needn't go for to frown at me that way. It makes no odds to me who's nabbed, and who ain't. The man's human, ain't he, and *could* be nabbed, I s'pose? I'm speaking for his own good, and you can take it or leave it.'

'I'll tell him what you say,' I answered curtly, and rode off, feeling vexed.

I did tell Zach; telling him, at the same time, that in my opinion Kappen was a jealous fool and only trying to make himself out important.

'Don't know so much about that,' said Zach. 'I've been

thinking the same myself about the Cove. It's getting a bit too well known, like. And though we brought it off with the cannon that time, I doubt if we could bring it off again. Maybe I will try another place or two for landing. Nights is long and dark now, so having a bit farther to carry overland won't make no odds.'

How bitterly afterwards I was to regret having said anything to Zach about Kappen's suggestion! Though, maybe, if the idea was in Zach's mind, too, it wouldn't have made any difference whether I had told him or not. Maybe what happened at Hey's Mouth one January night would have happened wherever Zach had landed.

I think, as long as I live, I shall not have done having nightmares about the events of that night. But, as I myself took no part in the initial events, except as an agonized spectator, I am going to set them down in Zach's own words, as I had them from his mouth afterwards.

16

Told by Zach Jewel

On the night of 18 January we had a fair run home from Roscoff, the night very dark, the wind sou'sou'west, a biggish sea running, and the *Little Peter* making good speed. About a mile off Hey's Mouth, where we were to make our landing (Jewel's Cove being too closely watched to be safe), the Revenue cutter, Captain John Hawkhurst, came out of the dark, nor' by east, and hailed us. And we making no answer, the cutter laid chase to us. I changed course, and thought to run out to sea again, but a burst of gunfire from the cutter brought down our fore mainsail all blazing, so we had to take and heave it overboard. I was loath to open fire on our side, lest we make matters worse for us if taken, and we made away as best we could, though crippled. But the cutter still firing, it wasn't long before the aft mainsail went the way of the other. And so, the cutter gaining on us, there was nothing for it but to open fire on our part. The night now lit up by gunfire, and the two vessels running close, I could see some fall wounded on both. But it was a doomed fight for us from the start, the cutter having the advantage of some powerful guns they had put on board for this night's work, and almost before we knew, we were grappled and boarded.

'This is good-bye to the *Little Peter* then,' thinks I, and resolved to sell my life dear, expecting no mercy, when I received a cut over the head and fell bleeding to the deck.

The next thing I knew, we were anchored in the bay, for they had taken the *Little Peter* in tow. I heard a trampling on the deck, and a voice say, 'Are the men secured below?'

'All but this poor fellow, and he's dead,' says another voice.

The first made answer, 'Put the man below.'

But the other said, 'What use to put a dead man below?'

And they both passed on.

So for a good two hours I lay there on my belly and in my blood, for my head was cut about shocking, and my nose all but severed in two. There was a sentinel kept walking past me, and once he stumbled over my feet, but

I lay as dead, and never stirred. Then comes another man with a lantern, and he takes hold of one of my legs, and lifts it, and lets it go again, and it drops like a stone back on the deck, for I was acting dead, and indeed I felt most like it. So then he puts his hand under my shirt, and says he, 'He's still warm, but his heart's stopped.' And so stoops with the lantern to have a look at my head. And, says he, 'His head is all to atoms.' So they passed, and left me lying.

The water was ebbing fast, and the *Little Peter*, being now grounded, was making a great heel to shore. There were two Revenue boats made fast alongside, and I heard a cry that one of them had broke adrift and was going out to sea. So then there was an order shouted to man the other boat and go after her. So, thinks I, now they are in this confusion, and their guard broke, now is the time to make my escape.

I began crawling along the deck on my belly, very slow and cautious, and got a kick from a man's heels that was about to drop overboard, but he did not notice me, so I lay quiet for a while, till they were all gone. Now, thinks I, if I can but get over the lee-side, I shall be able to swim ashore in a stroke or two.

I took hold of the burtons of the mast, and by that tackle began to lift myself over the side, when I was taken with a great cramp in one of my thighs. So, thinks I, I shall now drown, but still was willing to risk it, seeing naught else but to stay there and be hanged. So I let myself over the side by a rope into deep water.

I have but to swim a few strokes, thinks I. But I was that weak I began to sink like a stone, and the tide still running out swift, I was all the time hauling astern into deeper water. Now I gave up all hopes of life, for my head went under, and I began to swallow some water. But I had not lost my senses, for I found the rope still under my breast, and I began to haul on it, and it brought me up against the side where I went overboard, and there I held to it and stayed. I could not tell what best to do, whether to hail to the cutter's men to take me in, or to stay where I was and die, for my senses were now all but gone, and my strength also. So then, as I clung there, I came out of a kind of swound to find I was touching bottom with my feet. And with that my hope sprang up.

I began feeling about till I laid hold on another rope, leading towards the head of the vessel into shoaler water; and so, veering upon the one rope, and hauling upon the other, I came up under the bowsprit, and at times touched the sands of the sea with my feet. So I waited a little, and the tide ebbed away from my feet, and they were almost on the dry.

I let go the rope then, and thought to make a run for shore, but as soon as I tried to run, I fell down flat; and, as I fell, looking round about me, saw the shapes of three men standing close by. They were Excise men, watching for the boat, and they had not seen me. So I lay there quiet for some little time, till the men moved away, and then crept on my belly, I suppose about the distance of fifty yards. The ground was scuddy, flat rocks mixed with channels of sand, and ahead of me was a channel of white sand, showing up clear in the night.

If I am to creep over that, thinks I, 'twill take a goodish time, and I may be seen. So I got to my feet, to make a run for it, not knowing there was much amiss with me. But I found my mistake, for my legs gave under me, and there I was fallen down again.

Now on the shore, though I did not know it, were some of the Hey's Mouth fishermen, that Parson Lanyon had bid go down to see if they could pick up any of us, dead or alive. One of these men saw me fall, and ran and took me by the arm.

'Who are you?' says he.

I made no answer, taking him for an enemy.

'Have no fear,' says he very low. 'I'm a friend.'

Then came two more, which took me under both arms, and the other man pushed me in the back, and so were dragging me up the beach when I knew no more, for I fainted dead away.

17
Zach's Escape

Story continued by Dick Pellew

We who were waiting at Hey's Mouth for the *Little Peter* to come in had no thought, till we saw the gunfire, that anything was amiss. But at the first flash we knew that

Captain Hawkhurst had come up with our men. Still we had a hope that Zach would get away out to sea again, where, with his good seamanship and the speed of the *Little Peter*, it would be possible for him to dodge the Revenue cutter in the darkness, and maybe make back to Roscoff. But very soon we saw the *Little Peter* returning fire, and the rags of her sails floating ablaze on the water. And, at that sight, hope died within us.

'This is a sorry happening, Dick,' said Parson Lanyon, low in my ear.

I was too miserable to answer. I was thinking of Zach, and of what would be his fate, if he were taken.

The trouble that was upon all our spirits seemed darker than the night itself. The loaders, grouped together about us on the shore, were silent, except for a whispered exclamation now and then, or a muttered oath. Parson Lanyon turned to them and bid them get away with the donkeys into the thickets behind Hey's Mouth, and take the dapple mare and Diamond along with them, and there stay hid and quiet till we saw how things turned out. He and I stopped on the shore, and Roger Kappen, who had turned up from I don't know where, stood at our side.

'You best get away out of sight, my man,' said the parson to Kappen.

'Nay,' said Kappen. 'Why for? I'm a stranger in these parts, I am. There's naught known agin *me*. I can go where I've a mind to, and stop where I've a mind to; and if there's aught doing and I can lend a hand, so much the better.'

'That's true enough,' said the parson approvingly.

But I wished Kappen would go away. I felt like telling him he had no part nor lot in this affair. I felt like shouting at him, but I dared not open my mouth; for I was in that worked-up mood when I could have cursed anybody, the parson included. What was happening out there? Why wasn't I out there with them, to snatch up a pistol and blow Captain Hawkhurst's brains out? How was it with Zach?

'They're towing her in,' says Parson Lanyon, after a long silence. 'I'm afraid this is the end of the *Little Peter*. Dick, run up to the cottages, and bid any fishermen you can find there come down. Maybe we can save a few of our poor fellows yet.'

I did as he told me, glad to be doing anything. The fishermen came quickly and willingly enough, about half a dozen of them; though they had been hanging back till I gave them the parson's message, not wishing, as one of them explained, 'to be mixed up in no unpleasantness'. So then the parson and I went into hiding behind a little bank of sand and sea holly at the top of the shore, leaving these fishermen to watch, and bring us word when they had any news.

Hour after hour we lay hidden behind that sand-bank, with the roar of the sea in our ears, and the sand trickling into our faces and down our necks whenever we moved. Now and then the parson would whisper something to me, but I had no answers for him. In fact, I didn't hear what he said. My thoughts were with Zach, and my mind in agony. If only I could be doing something – anything! But I could do nothing but crouch there and wait. By and by, raising my head above the bank, I saw the *Little Peter* close inshore, with the light of a lantern wavering to and fro along her deck, and the dim bulk of the Revenue cutter farther out, with one white light at her masthead.

Everything was deadly quiet, except for the roaring of the sea – that old familiar sound that was never out of our ears, day or night, whatever might be happening, whether we were merry or sad, whether men lived or died. And then, suddenly, came a shout of a boat gone adrift, and some loudly spoken orders, and the sight of the lantern on the *Little Peter* swung out over the bowsprit, and so disappearing. And after that the sound of oars. And then nothing again but the roaring of the sea.

I don't know how long it would be after this – for time was standing still for me, and I had my face in my hands, trying vainly to blot out the ghastly pictures that kept flashing through my mind – when Parson Lanyon gave an exclamation and scrambled up out of the sand.

'They're bringing someone up!' he said, and began running down the beach, quite oblivious of any danger to himself.

I ran after him. Three men were coming towards us, carrying a fourth.

'Who is it?' said the parson.

'I think 'tis Zach Jewel, sir,' says one of the men.

'Not – dead?' whispered Parson Lanyon.

'If he's breathing, 'tis all he is,' answered the man.

They carried Zach up into one of the cottages, and I helped them, my hands all sticky with his blood. The window being well screened, a woman brought a candle, and we laid Zach on the floor, and a man took the candle and kneeled beside him. I saw him plainly then; but he was so cut about the face and head that all I knew him by was his hands and his kersey overcoat. We stripped off his wet clothes, and wrapped him in blankets, and the woman and Parson Lanyon cleaned up his wounds as best they could.

'The bone of his nose is cut right in two,' said the parson. 'We'll have to get a doctor to him.'

And just then another man ran in, and told us

that some of the Hawkhurst's men were coming up the shore.

'Then we must get him out of here,' says the parson. 'For by all that's holy they shan't take him! Is there a back way out of this cottage?'

There was a back way, through a door in a little scullery; and that way we carried Zach, and through a bit of garden, and up to the thickets where the men and donkeys were still waiting. And all this time Zach lay as one dead, and I thought never to hear him speak or laugh again. Parson Lanyon bid the men get the donkeys away home as best they might, and asked for volunteers among the fishermen to carry Zach to the parsonage. They were all willing, and two of them went back to the cottages and fetched a sail and some spars, and out of these made a stretcher, and laid Zach on it. And so we set out, the parson riding his mare and leading Diamond, and the rest of us carrying the stretcher, trying to bear it smoothly. But, in the darkness and over the rough ground we had to travel, poor Zach got many a jolt, and it was only by miracle, it seemed to me, that we did not drop him.

We got away none too soon, for we heard afterwards that the Excise men searched all the cottages, and were mighty suspicious when they found a woman down on her knees mopping up her kitchen floor by candlelight. What excuse she made, I don't know; but I do know that neither threats nor coaxings could get the truth out of her.

At the parsonage we made up a bed for Zach in the parlour, for we dared not risk carrying him upstairs. Jimmy Bandy rode off for Doctor Treglown, who came and asked no questions, but set the bone in Zach's nose, stitched up his other wounds, and shook his head over him.

'Will he do?' asked Parson Lanyon.

'Can't say yes, can't say no,' answered Doctor Treglown. 'His skull is badly fractured.'

'It must be yes!' said the parson.

And just then, as if he had heard him, Zach opened his eyes, and gave a kind of smile; and though he immediately became unconscious again, I could have shouted for joy. For surely he was saying 'yes' himself!

In the morning we had sad news, brought by that officious fellow, Roger Kappen, whom I detested for being the bearer of it. Some of the men had made their escape, but some had been killed. Matthy and Job were taken, and there was a reward of £300 offered for Zach's apprehension.

'Then he can't stay here, that's certain,' said Parson Lanyon. 'It's too near his home. And though there's not a man, woman, or child in the seven parishes will give him away, Hawkhurst's fellows will have a search-warrant for all the houses hereabouts. What shall we do with him, Dick?'

'There are the garrets at Pellew House,' I said. 'And I'll lock the door at the top of the garret stairs, and sit behind it day and night with a gun.'

'No, my boy,' said the parson with a smile. 'That's not very practicable. We must think of something better.'

'There's the hut on Trevy Downs,' said Kappen.

'The very place!' exclaimed the parson. 'We'll get him up there tonight.'

'I could bring the sledge for him,' said Kappen.

I didn't think it the very place, because I was jealous that Kappen had suggested it. Everything to do with that fellow I disliked and distrusted.

'The sledge will jolt him to pieces,' I objected.

'We'll pad him round with pillows,' said the parson. 'It's the best we can do.'

Zach was still unconscious; but when Doctor Treglown came that morning, he said Zach was 'holding his own', that his breathing was stronger, and that he thought he would pull through. He looked shrewdly at the parson, and his little grey eyes twinkled.

'I'm not sure whether I heard the fellow's name,' he said, 'and certainly if I did, I don't remember it. Nor is it possible to recognize a face so damaged. To a medical man, a patient is a patient, anonymous or otherwise. I ask no questions. But I hear rumours of a search-warrant and other unpleasantnesses. And if – I don't say it's likely – but *if* a search-party should stray this way, it would be as well that they should find the parsonage unencumbered.'

'It's all arranged,' answered Parson Lanyon. 'I shan't ask you to come here again.'

'Excellent!' said Doctor Treglown. 'But the patient will still require a doctor.'

'Would the doctor submit to being blindfolded, for his own peace of mind?' asked Parson Lanyon.

Doctor Treglown's little grey eyes twinkled more brightly than ever. 'A bandage over his eyes is an excellent remedy for a nervous headache,' he said.

After the doctor had gone, Parson Lanyon said, 'In a moment of petulance, Dick, I once called Treglown an ass. I take back those words as unchristian and not to the point. What *is* to the point is that Treglown is an admirable fellow.'

And I, who had never thought the doctor an ass, agreed heartily.

That was an anxious day. For one thing, Zach never stirred nor opened his eyes, and to see him there, lying like a fallen log, as if he would never move again, smote me to the heart. And then we were in a state of tension, and continually on the watch for the Excise men; for we could not move Zach before dark, and what to do or say if the Excise men arrived and demanded entrance, we could not think. We heard that they had been up at Jewel's Place, and that Gracie Winkey had so screamed down her curses upon them, and so terrified them by the plagues she was about to smite them with, that they had turned tail and ridden away.

'Why didn't I think of getting the witch down here?' said Parson Lanyon. 'She's a surer defence than any number of cannon.'

But then news was brought that Hawkhurst himself had been up at Jewel's Place, quite unperturbed by all that Gracie Winkey might threaten him with, or by the combined ravings of Sarah and Zeb. He had made a thorough search, so it was said, but there was nothing to discover: Job and Matthy being already in custody, and Harry gone, nobody knew where.

We were still discussing this piece of news, when the parson's housekeeper came in. She looked frightened.

'Captain Hawkhurst's at the door, sir,' she said, 'and would like to speak to you.'

Parson Lanyon immediately dropped into an armchair, and closed his eyes. 'You know that I am very unwell, Molly,' he said in a weak voice. 'And, in fact, I had to send for Doctor Treglown. The doctor suspects that I have contracted smallpox, and has absolutely forbidden me to see anyone. Pray take the Captain my excuses. I should not like,' said the parson with a groan, 'to be the unhappy cause of contaminating His Majesty's Excise.'

'No, sir,' says Molly, 'I'll tell the Captain, sir.'

'I fear I have lengthened my term in Purgatory by yet another lie, Dick,' said Parson Lanyon, when Molly had left the room. 'Or will the Lord take motives into account, think you?'

'I'm sure He will,' I said, as I peeped from behind the window curtain, and watched Captain Hawkhurst ride slowly away.

'What troubles me most about that lie,' said the parson, getting up to walk restlessly about the room, 'is that it may prove ineffective; and that we may have Hawkhurst back again.'

'Hardly today, sir,' I said, for the light was already fading. 'And tomorrow he can walk through all your rooms, for Zach will not be here.'

We sat impatiently waiting for night, doing from time to time such little things for Zach as the doctor had ordered. Once, after I had put into his mouth a few drops from some concoction in a bottle, he opened his eyes wide and stared at me perplexedly.

'Dick?' he said, in a husky whisper, and tried to smile, and shut his eyes again. And I was so overcome that I knelt at his side and thanked God for this great mercy. As for Parson Lanyon, he first began to dance an absurd jig, laughing and snapping his fingers, and then sat down and wept, with his face in his hands. And then started up again, and ran out into the night (for it was now dark) to listen for the sound of Kappen's sledge.

'He's come, Dick! Kappen's come!' said he, hurrying in a few minutes later. And he began gathering up cushions from sofa and chairs, and darted out again with an armful of them. But I stayed at Zach's side, hoping that he might open his eyes and speak to me again.

Between us, when all was ready, Kappen and I and Jimmy Bandy carried Zach out and laid him in the sledge, which was piled high with cushions and with the pillows which Molly had brought from upstairs. Then, having covered Zach over with blankets, we set out on our long, slow journey up to Trevy Downs, leaving the parson reluctantly behind. For, as he explained, since he was suffering from smallpox, it would be best for him to be home, and safely tucked up in bed, in case Hawkhurst should decide to risk the infection and pay him another visit.

18

Refuge with the Tinners

It took us getting on for three hours to reach the hut on Trevy Downs, for though the distance from the parsonage was not much over five miles, the going was exceedingly rough. We dared not show a light, and in the intense darkness of the winter night we had to pause often to take our bearings. Great boulders seemed to rise up from nowhere and bar our way, and there were wildernesses of furze and dead bracken to be got round, and bogs to avoid, and overgrown deserted mine-workings (death traps for the unwary), and the stream leats of the tin-streamers branching in all directions to cut us off. And though I thought I knew every inch of that wild country, I found I was mistaken. The guide whom I had so blithely followed on previous dark nights up there, was now lying helpless to aid us, and without him it seemed that I was all at sea.

Jimmy Bandy knew less of the way than I did; and it was Roger Kappen who, surprisingly, took the lead and steered us, though with some hesitations, among the bewilderment of pitfalls.

'Have you been up here often, then?' I asked.

'But once, Dick,' said he. 'And that by daylight after rabbits. But once is enough for a man with eyes in his head.'

Since this seemed to imply that I had not eyes in my head, I felt offended, and did not answer.

'And speaking of eyes, now,' went on Kappen. 'Of course, we're doing all we can, but between you and me, Dick, it ain't no manner of use. This here poor friend of yours is doomed, just as sure as if Cap'n Hawkhurst had him atween his talons. And if he ain't got him atween his talons already, that's because he's biding his time, as I told 'ee before. Aye, we can hide the poor worm here, and we can hide the poor worm there, but the hawk'll pounce, Dick, for his eyes is sharp, and he's got more eyes than his own to help him over this job, I reckon. Or how come he knew 'bout the landing at Hey's Mouth?'

'But that was your suggestion!' I burst out wildly.

'Nay, Dick, give a man his due,' answered Kappen. '*I* said naught 'bout Hey's Mouth. All *I* did say was take and land some other place, and change that place often. And that were good counsel, though it fell out badly, more's the pity. You ain't blaming old Roger for that, surely?'

'I don't know,' I muttered. 'I don't know who's to blame.'

'Nor don't any man,' said Kappen. 'Who can it be, Dick? One of your friend's crew, would you say now? One as took fright and thought to save his own skin, and gain a bit of money, maybe. Men'll do a lot to save their skin, and they'll do a lot for money, too. Not the likes of me and you wouldn't, but there's some as will.'

I couldn't bear it. I found myself stamping my foot at him. Wasn't it enough, I said, that we were in all this trouble, without his rubbing it in? Why did he take this delight in tormenting me? 'Oh, I'll own you're helping us,' I cried, 'but I could almost wish it was any one but you!'

'And that's not civil nor sensible of 'ee, Dick,' says he. 'For it seems I'm the only one as knows the way we're going in this darkness.'

The hut lay in a big hollow among the moors, with a wide clearing of trampled earth and coarse grass all round it, and a stream, with frequent dams, meandering through the clearing. We came to it at last, and I was indeed heartened by the warm glow of firelight showing through one of the loopholes near the chimney end – most of the others being blocked up with wads of rushes and bracken to keep out the cold. I gave the whistle which was the smugglers' signal, and the low door was immediately opened by a little shaggy-headed tinner, all knobs and bumps like a gnome.

'Come away in, boys,' said he, 'and be sharp about it. 'Tis a wisht look-out for 'ee by all accounts.'

'We've got Zach Jewel here,' said I, 'and he's sorely wounded.'

'Zach Jewel?' At the news some dozen men came thronging to the doorway. 'Zach, do 'ee say? ... Ah, we'd gove him up for dead! ... Bring un in, the poor of un! ... Easy now, soft and suant ... Here, lay un down afore the fire, that's the way of it ... My days, look on his face! ... 'Tis Zach hisself, you do say? ... Well, who'd 'a known it! ... Would a drop of brandy help? No? Well, you know best what doctor do say ... Just let un lie quiet, is it? ... Gor! I wouldn't have had this happen for a fortune! ... Will he live, then? ... Well, that's something!'

They were all in a bustle of solicitude and kindness, tossing aside their wet boots that were drying before the fire, and heaping up a great bed of fern for Zach to lie on, urging brandy upon *us*, since they might not give it to Zach. I was fairly overcome, and what with my weariness, and the tension of the last three hours out there in the darkness, and the relief of having got Zach into shelter at last, I could scarce utter a word to speak my thankfulness.

Kappen and Jimmy Bandy soon took themselves off with the sledge and the black horse and the greater number of the cushions; though I kept a couple of pillows to put under Zach's head, and the blankets to cover him. One of the tinners offered himself as a guide off the moor, but this offer Kappen refused.

'I found my ways up, and I can find my ways down,' he said, somewhat ungraciously.

As for myself, I was staying there. I was not going to leave Zach, and I relied on Parson Lanyon to convey the tidings to my father, in whatever way he thought best.

'We've got a surprise for 'ee,' said an old tin-streamer, whose name was Tom Treva. 'I wasn't saying nothing afore he with the yaller face took hisself off, because you never know. Harry's down below.'

'What! Harry Jewel!'

'That's of it,' said Tom. 'He gave a jump overboard and

swam ashore soon arter the firing began last night. And he brast in here like a risen ghost. Says he, "There's not a man living from off'n the *Little Peter* but only me!" Howsomever, there's talk of some in hiding in the tunnel down at Jewel's Place, and they'll be dropping in when they see their way clear, I shouldn't wonder. Ought us to put Zach below, think 'ee?'

'Nay, leave un bide where he is till morning,' said another. 'He's had handling enough.'

'Then us could fetch Harry up to un, I s'pose?' said Tom. 'He'll be skeered like, maybe, wondering what's doing up over his head. Aye, he's much like a rat in a trap down there, though us made un as comfortable as us could.'

He took down a lantern from a hook on the wall, moved aside some bundles of faggots from beside the hearth, stooped through the little door, and disappeared, leaving the company with the firelight flickering on their faces. There were old men and young men, some bearded, some with a week's growth of stubble, mostly small, lean and wiry, short-legged, and with arms powerfully muscled, all of them unwashed and plastered with reddish mud: a wild-looking, harsh-featured crew, but more to me than a company of angels would have been, because of their concern for Zach's welfare. Three hundred pounds for Zach, indeed! If it had been three million, I knew that not one of these men would have deigned to fall for it.

Very soon the little door behind the faggot pile was pushed open again, and Tom Treva crawled out, followed by Harry Jewel.

'Where is he?' cried Harry wildly. 'Oh, Zach, my brother! My brother, Zach! I never thought to see thee more!' And there he was slumped down on the fern beside Zach, and shaking with sobs. ''Tisn't Zach,' cried he, 'and yet 'tis Zach! And I'm shamed to have left 'ee, Zach, when it was more fit I put my body in front of yourn!'

'There now, wisht, Harry,' said an old man. ''Twouldn't have made no difference, 'cept that you'd not be here, but most like stiff and dead.'

But Harry was not to be consoled, and kept on sobbing out how he'd deserted Zach, till he sobbed himself to sleep, with his head against Zach's unconscious body.

So the night passed away. The tinners drew an iron bar across the door, and laid them down to sleep: one across the doorway, the others sprawled anywhere about the floor on beds of fern, with rolled-up coats for pillows, and their guns handy. I had no thought of sleep. I sat at Zach's side, watching the blazing up and dying down of the logs in the great chimney, hearing the snores and heavy breathing of the sleepers, and thinking I know not what of dazed and muddled thoughts. I felt I would never sleep again: and then, suddenly, I *was* asleep, and struggling with terrifying nightmares – and woke with a start to hear Zach talking. And the wild way the words came out of him, and the nonsense he talked, and the surprise of it, was even more terrifying than the nightmares; for it seemed my nightmares were nothing in comparison with his.

What ought I to do? I dripped some of the doctor's medicine into his mouth, and took his hand, and began talking in my turn: put my mouth close to his ear, and told him he was safe among friends, and getting well, and that it was I, Dick, and that he had only to rest, only to rest ... And by and by he was quiet again; and then I got into a panic that he was now dead, and that I couldn't hear his breathing. Altogether, I was in a sorry state before a blink of wintry greyness showed through the unblocked loophole, and I knew that it was dawn.

It was still quite dark in the hut, except for the red glow of the dying fire; but, with that first blink of dawn, there was a great stir among the tinners. The fire was soon roaring with fresh faggots, a huge kettle hung over it, and quantities of tea brewed. And so, having swallowed down a breakfast of cold meat and bread and tea, the tinners put on their coats and boots, collected their hats and candles, picks and other gear, and prepared to set out for their day's work; most of them for Treva mine, but a few of the older ones to sieve the tin out of the stream beds.

Before they went, they carried Zach, with great care and gentleness, down into the huge cellar under the hut, and there laid him on a fresh bed of fern, and covered him over with the parson's blankets. Harry Jewel and I were to stay down there with him, and they gave us a lantern and quantities of food. Old Tom Treva announced that he would do no stream work that day, but stop on guard in the hut, and bar the door behind the others; and he sent his grandson, Sammy, who worked with him, to fetch Doctor Treglown.

I was up and down between the cellar and the hut a dozen times, watching for the doctor's coming. And when he came, it was a laughable sight. Sammy had gone off on foot, but he returned riding the doctor's horse, and the doctor sat up behind him, rigid as a poker, with a handkerchief bound over his eyes, his two arms wound tightly round Sammy's waist, and his two hands clasping his bag.

'Are we arrived then at last?' he said, when Sammy pulled up outside the door of the hut. 'Never in all my days have I had a ride like this, so bumped and jolted and flung around like a sack of turnips! And where we are now, I cannot imagine! Is that Dick Pellew's voice I hear?

Help me down, Dick, for mercy's sake! Lead me where you will – but get me off this animal!'

I gave him my hand, set him on his feet, and led him in. But it is my opinion that he knew well enough where he was, and could see well enough through the handkerchief, too. For he bowed his head through the low doorway, and marched across the hut, avoiding every obstacle and every unevenness of the littered floor. Still, the pretence of being blindfolded must be kept up. At the little door behind the faggot pile, I warned him to watch his steps.

'Watch my steps, Dick Pellew!' he exclaimed. 'And how do you expect me to do that? Watch them for me, if you don't wish me to be laid up beside my patient with a broken leg! Heaven preserve us! It seems we are descending a flight of stairs!'

With a great show of feeling with his feet, and groping with his hands, I got him down into the cellar, and untied the handkerchief from round his eyes.

Immediately all the jocular pretence fell from him. He became swift and precise and almost stern. Without one glance at Harry or Tom Treva, whom, of course, he knew well, but preferred to ignore, he opened his bag, spread out his instruments, felt Zach's pulse, listened to his heart-beats, had me running for hot water, and 'any kind of bowl I could lay hands on,' told me that if I fainted he would consider me not worth my salt, rolled up Zach's sleeve, and bled him.

I couldn't help feeling that Zach had lost enough blood already from his wounds; but it seemed Doctor Treglown knew best, for very soon after this, Zach opened his eyes, and spoke the first sensible words I had heard him utter since his rescue.

'Where be I?' he said, in a weak, pitiful whisper.

'I haven't the faintest idea,' said Doctor Treglown. 'Speak to him, Dick, and put his mind at ease.'

And with that he walked off to the other end of the cellar, and, hands behind back, became absorbed in the contemplation of some brandy casks.

I stooped at Zach's side, and told him he was safe among friends in Treva hut, and that Harry was here with him. 'You've been wounded, Zach,' I said, 'but you're mending fast, and Doctor Treglown is seeing to you.'

Zach's eyes closed. His eyes and mouth were all I could see of his face, swathed as it was in bandages. When his eyes opened again there was such a bewilderment and trouble in them as smote me to the heart.

'The – rest –' he muttered. 'What –'

I knew what he wanted to ask – and I didn't know how to answer him. But, at that moment, Doctor Treglown, who, I am sure, had heard every word I said, turned from his contemplation of the brandy casks and came striding back across the cellar.

'Now my unknown patient,' said he briskly, 'we have to dress those cuts of yours; and I give you warning it's going to hurt. Mix some brandy and water for him, Dick. That's right! Here man, gollup it down – and for mercy's sake hold the lantern closer, somebody – this place is as black as the pit!'

The dressing of his wounds sent Zach unconscious again, but not for long. Doctor Treglown seemed very well satisfied, told Zach he had the constitution of a Hercules, and at last demanded that he himself be blindfolded again, 'led out of this infernal den', and taken home.

'As he goes through life, Dick, a man finds himself in some curious situations,' he remarked, as I helped him on to the horse behind Sammy. 'But of all the – Well, there, never, mind. Is that my bag you're putting into my hands? Let me keep a tight hold of that, if of nothing else, in this crazy world! And it seems I shall have to repeat the mad performance tomorrow, and for many tomorrows! However, the patient – whoever he may be – is doing well, and that's all that should concern the doctor.'

19

Urgent Business with Lord Trembath

Zach continued to do well, but the gaining of strength was a slow process. However, he was by and by sufficiently recovered to get up the cellar stairs sometimes, with a strong arm to support him, and we began to discuss our next move. For he could not stay in hiding for ever, and there seemed only one thing to be done, though I hated the thought of it, and that was to smuggle him out of England as soon as he was fit enough. Hawkhurst was still actively on the search for him, and for any others of the crew of the *Little Peter* who might be still lurking in the neighbourhood. But, bribe and cajole and threaten as he would, he could get no information out of anyone – only blank looks and obstinate head-shakings.

We were becoming quite a large company in the cellar. The men who had been hiding in the tunnel at Jewel's Place came 'dropping in', as Tom Treva had foretold, making their way up over the moors by night, sometimes two together, but more often singly. These men, though confined below on the *Little Peter* when she was anchored in Hey's Mouth, owed their escape to the guard being relaxed during the confusion over the cutter's boat – and most like to the kindly feelings of that guard, for not all Hawkhurst's men were as fiercely convinced of their duty as he was himself.

Three of the neighbouring gentry's sons had been packed off with extraordinary expedition on a tour of Europe 'to complete their education'; and though Hawkhurst might suspect the reason for their sudden going, they were safe from his clutches. Les Skewish and Digory Whear had boldly gone back to work, looking, and not in vain, to Farmer Trevillian and Lord Trembath to protect them. What would Hawkhurst have? So far as their employers knew, these two men had been sleeping in their beds like honest fellows on the night of the run; and, since Hawkhurst could not prove otherwise, he was obliged to let them alone. But there were four men killed, and in mourning their loss we one and all branded Hawkhurst as their murderer.

And we had bad news of Matthy and Job Jewel. Hawkhurst, knowing better than to have them brought to trial in their native county, had them carried up into Devonshire, where they now lay in Exeter jail, awaiting trial.

We had bad news of the *Little Peter*, too. All the discoverable contraband had, of course, been taken out of her; that was to be expected. But what sadly distressed us was that Hawkhurst had then ordered her to be blown up. And now all that was left of that brave little vessel was a scatter of fragments drifting in the shallows off Hey's Mouth. It seemed to me like the murder of a living soul.

As I could do nothing useful any longer by staying mewed up in the hut, and, on the other hand, might pick up scraps of news by being abroad, I went back home: and it was I who now brought the blindfolded Doctor Treglown up on his ever-less-frequent visits to attend to Zach. By the time those visits stopped I had learned the intricacies of the way so thoroughly that I think I could have taken the journey blindfolded myself.

'You know, I have been having a most peculiar dream,' said the doctor, one night, when I had set him down at his own door and taken the bandage from his eyes for the last time. 'But, praise be to Heaven, I am now awake, and it is curious how swiftly the details of a dream are expunged from the waking memory. I seem, in some kind of a nightmare, to have been attending a badly wounded man in a dark cellar, the man and the location equally unknown to me. But that, of course, is all nonsense.'

'Of course,' I answered gravely. 'But if it were *not* nonsense, I, for one, should like to thank you.'

'Nonsense!' repeated Doctor Treglown. 'All nonsense, I assure you.'

I continued my visits to the hut by night, and it was surprising to me how often, either going or returning, I fell in with Roger Kappen. Once I nearly fell over him, as he was crouched in the dark beside a furze bush not far from the hut. I asked him what he was doing there.

'Anxious I be, Dick,' he said. 'A man has his natural

feelings. There's quite a company in that there cellar now, by all accounts, what with Harry Jewel and the rest. Things will get abroad you know, one way or t'other. But don't you fret yourself. Roger Kappen's deep and secret as the bottom of the Bay of Biscay. A friend on the watch, that's what I be, although you be all bent on holding of me off.'

But I did fret myself. It was not at all to my liking that Kappen should know about 'Harry Jewel and the rest'. How should he know? To my certain knowledge he had never been inside the hut, for the tinners were a close and jealous community, and they trusted no outsider. There was some mystery about this I could not explain, and I remembered uneasily the men's talk about a 'tongue-tabbas'.

Meanwhile, Parson Lanyon had got news of a ship leaving St Mewes for Brittany, whose captain was willing to risk the carrying of our men with him. This was good news. But when I called on Doctor Treglown to consult him about the possibility of moving Zach, he shook his head most emphatically.

'As I remember that dream man,' he said, 'I felt him requiring no further medical attention, but still extremely weak. It would be sheer madness, always supposing that such a man really existed, to send him on a rough sea voyage, and land him in heaven knows what primitive and insanitary lodging at this time of the year.'

So Zach must stay behind, and Harry refused to leave him. But the rest of the men set out for St Mewes on a moonless night, and were smuggled into the hold of the ship, and carried across the water to safety, and that was something.

Zach made light of their going. 'So long, boys,' he said, as he bid them good-bye. 'There'll be a pretty company of us over to Roscoff presently – a home from home that place'll be. And I wouldn't say but what we'll pick up a bit of trade there, neither.'

Yes, he made light of it, but I knew he must be sore at heart, both for their sakes and his own; for the destruction of the *Little Peter*, too, the present ruin of all his ventures, and for the probable fate of Job and Matthy.

But we had not much time for dwelling on our troubles. The very next night after the men had gone (and a wild night it was, black, with gusts of rain, and a strong wind blowing), there came a whistle at the hut door, and when it was opened in burst Digory Whear. He was spattered with mud, he was scratched and bleeding, and fetching his breath in great gasps.

'Get Zach and Harry out of here!' he gasped. 'Hawkhurst's got word of where they're to, and he's coming – they'm on their way now, men, hosses, and guns. I passed 'em in the darkness; they was casting round for a path among the bogs, and I heaved a stone or two and brought one down; they shot off a gun, but it missed me – oh, for the Lord's sake, for the Lord's sake, get them two out of here!'

Our first thought was to fight it out, knowing our strength inside that granite hut. The tinners were already pulling the wads of rush and bracken out of the loophole windows, and priming their guns, when Zach stopped them.

'I'm having no more men killed for me,' he said. 'I'll give myself up sooner.'

Zach give himself up indeed! As if anyone would agree to that! And it was Tom Treva who hit upon another idea: Harry and I were to get away with Zach over the moors to the north and make for Lord Trembath's place. Once we got there, I was to act as ambassador, get private word with Lord or Lady Trembath, and explain the whole affair. 'They'll make 'ee welcome, never fear,' said Digory.

Meanwhile the tinners would delay Hawkhurst by making a ring of fire round the hut, a fire so big that, while it lasted, neither men nor horses could pass through it.

The idea was no sooner suggested than it was acted on. You will remember that the hut stood in a wide clearing threaded by a stream within a hollow in the moors. While the three of us, with Zach swaying on his feet, and Harry and I grasping him by either arm, groped our way in the wind and darkness out of the hollow, the tinners were hurrying with huge bundles of furze and faggots across the stream to set them up all round the edges of the clearing. Looking back, as we reached the top of the hollow, I saw a ring of little leaping lights where the tinners had kindled the furze, and then suddenly, a great blaze of golden flames that soared heavenward, fanned by the strong wind, amid a roar of the burning furze and a crackling and smoke-belching from the kindling faggots.

The flames rose higher and higher; they lit the moors for a mile round, and that was something we had not reckoned on. They made us all too visible, and they guided Hawkhurst and his men on their way as surely as a welcoming beacon. I could see them coming along the flat of the moor, with their black shadows wavering behind them, and the light catching on their stirrups and belts and the buttons of their coats. But it seemed that they had not seen us, for they rode directly up to the ring of fire, and there they scattered, this way and that, seeking for a way through it.

We heard afterwards that the tinners made a great show of fright, screeching out that they would be burnt alive, and calling on the Excise men to come through the fire and rescue them. What Hawkhurst made of this pantomime I don't know, but the dawn was up and we were far away before the fire had died down and he could leap his horse over the hot ashes and demand that Zach should be brought out and handed over to him. And then, of course, nobody knew what he was talking about, for Zach was not there, nor had anyone heard news of him. And Hawkhurst had to ride back the way he had come, in a very ill temper.

Dawn found us still far from Lord Trembath's, and we had to lie all that day secreted under great slabs of rock on the earthy floor of one of the 'giants' houses', as we called them – one of those mysterious, prehistoric graves with which the moors abounded. It was perhaps just as well we had to stop, for Zach was exhausted, and we had no sooner crawled into our hiding-place than he fell fast asleep, and slept the day through, while Harry and I kept uneasy watch. But we saw nothing more alarming than a ruddy-cheeked fox, that came nosing round the stones like a dog, and galloped away at the scent of us; and we heard nothing but the crying of the peewits and the monotonous dry rustle of the wind through the lean grass.

The dusk fell early on that gloomy winter day, and by five o'clock in the afternoon we thought it safe to wake Zach and set out once more. The wind was behind us and sped us on our way, and in the early hours of the morning we were clear of the moors and on a path between high hedges that brought us to the gates of Bosnahallon, Lord Trembath's place. It was not safe to wait for daylight; so, having left Zach and Harry hidden in a ditch, I boldly marched up the ilex avenue, crossed the sward in front of the house, and pulled on the bell under the gatehouse so vigorously that I startled myself by the clamour I made.

I startled the household, too. But, on announcing my name, and stating that I had urgent business with Lord Trembath, I was brought within by one goggle-eyed serving-man, while another went to summon his lordship.

'Is it war with France again, Dick, that you so rudely rouse an old fellow from his sleep?' said that genial gentleman, shuffling down into the hall in his bedgown and nightcap, with rabbitskin slippers flapping on his gouty feet.

'Not that I know of, sir,' I answered. 'But I am in dire need of help.'

I told him everything; and, without any ado, he bid me fetch in Zach and Harry, had a fire kindled in a room in an empty wing of the great house, and mattresses laid on the floor, promising there should be beds on the morrow. All this as a matter of course, without fuss and without question, only demanding why on earth we hadn't come to him long ago.

'No one will trouble us here,' he said, 'we're too far from the coast. And, as for you, my lad, you best get a good sleep yourself, for you look at the end of your tether.'

And he had me brought to a pleasant bedroom near to his own, where I pulled off my boots and coat, got under the covers, and fell at once into a sleep of sheer exhaustion.

20

Condemned to Death

It was past noon when I woke to a cold and glittering day, with a grey-bird singing wildly on a leafless sycamore outside the window, and in myself a grateful feeling that most of our troubles were over. Lady Trembath had meanwhile been in to see Zach, and, finding him weak, had insisted on sending for a young doctor from St Mewes, who came very willingly and openly – ostensibly to attend on her ladyship, who found herself conveniently a little indisposed, but in reality to see Zach.

I left for home with a light heart that afternoon, riding a borrowed horse, and promising myself that I would return the horse and pay Zach a visit next morning; which I did, and found him cheerful, and looking forward to the day when he and Harry would be able to get across to Roscoff and join the others. But Lady Trembath, who was enjoying her role of conspirator, said he must not think of it for many weeks to come.

At home, my father raised his eyebrows at me, and said he was gratified to have me sleeping under the parental roof once more; though he understood that a young fellow of my age must be allowed to amuse himself from time to time away from home.

'I was the same myself, Dick, in my youth,' he said. 'Though I don't know that I went courting at quite such a tender age. However,' said he, with that thin, flickering smile of his, 'I shall be pleased to welcome her – when you have made up your mind.'

Courting indeed! I had graver matters on my mind than that nonsense, as he very well knew, but would not admit.

The gravest of all, now that Zach was safe, was the fate of Job and Matthy. When the day of the trial drew near, I could not rest, but set off to ride into Devonshire, taking Neil with me, partly for company, and also because it had become my practice now to keep an eye on him when I could. We put up in Exeter at a quiet inn near the court-house, and I found the city buzzing with sympathy for the smugglers, over whom there was a deal of head-shaking, for the judge was reputed to be a stern man, and an 'upright', in his own interpretation of the word. However, it was thought that the jury would be sympathetic to the accused, and that gave me hope.

On the day of the trial I hung about, amid a great crowd, outside the court (for I thought it best to remain inconspicuous); and, as the weary hours passed, was tormented with conflicting rumours. Now it was said that there was no hope for the prisoners; now that the defending lawyer (whose fees were paid by anonymous donors in Cornwall) had made such a passionate speech in their favour that they were as good as free men; now, again, that the judge was in a bad temper, and conviction was sure. In the late afternoon, being parched with thirst, and dizzy with apprehension, I went into a near-by ale house, but had scarce raised the glass to my lips, when I heard a great roar from the crowd outside.

I set down my glass and ran, to find myself in the midst of a riot: the trial was over, the prisoners were convicted, the sentence was death – the judge adding insult to injury by reminding poor Job and Matthy that it was open to them to receive a free pardon, nay, and a reward into the bargain, should they feel inclined to reveal the names and whereabouts of two, or more, of their accomplices.

The city was in an uproar. But of what use, now, to smash windows and throw stones – how would that help? Sick at heart, I returned on my melancholy journey, my spirits utterly weighed down with Job's and Matthy's fate, and the thought of having to convey the news to Zach. But when I visited him at Bosnahallon, I found him already acquainted with it, for the news had spread, it seemed, more swiftly than I could travel. He was thoughtful, but not so downcast as I had expected.

'Dick,' said he, 'you're not as old as some, but you've got more strength in you than many a man, and sense and pluck added. You once did a brave job for us. Can you find it in your heart to do another?'

'You know I will do anything in my power, Zach,' I said.

'Could you get permission, think you, for you and one other, to pay our poor boys a farewell visit?'

'Why yes, I believe it is allowed,' I said.

'Then we'll have them free, Dick, by Golles, we'll have

them free,' cried Zach, slapping his two hands to his thighs and stooping forward (a characteristic attitude of his) to look at me with dancing eyes. 'Harry here is mad to go with 'ee, but I doubt that's not safe.'

'I could, with a disguise on me,' pleaded Harry. 'Leave me go, Zach. I owe it to them and you.'

'But how can anyone visiting them set them free?' I asked.

'With guns and good horses, and a turnkey friendly like as not,' said Zach, 'it shouldn't be too difficult.'

I began to understand, and my heart swelled with pride that such a task should be entrusted to me. We took Lady Trembath into our confidence, for we must have somewhere to bring the rescued men to, if we *could* rescue them, and the idea that we might fail didn't so much as enter my mind. Lady Trembath was still a youngish woman, and delighted to share in the plot.

'For two pins,' said she, 'I'd dress me up as a sailor and come along with you – only I expect his lordship would have something to say.'

Lord Trembath had 'married beneath him', as they say, and his lady had been an actress before she wed. Now her experience came in useful. She said of course Harry should go with me, and she would so disguise him that even his own mother wouldn't recognize him.

'He shall be a sailor with rings in his ears,' she said, 'and the tarriest of tarry pigtails, and we'll give him some curly whiskers – grey whiskers, I think – oh, and there must be streaks of silver in his black hair, and some strong, middle-aged lines on his handsome face. And if you could stoop your shoulders a little, my man – well, no, it will be safer to pad them.'

And off she danced, to ask Lord Trembath to apply for the necessary permit for 'an uncle and nephew of the prisoners' to come and take leave of their poor condemned relatives.

'You know, my dear,' said Lord Trembath, 'this takes some consideration. If *I* were to make the application, and there were to be hue and cry after the escaped prisoners, the first place the searchers would make for would be Bosnahallon. It wouldn't be safe, in that case, to bring them here.'

'But they must come here!' said Lady Trembath.

'Then somebody else must make the application,' said Lord Trembath.

I thought of my father. Would he do it? Yes, I believed he would; for whatever pretences he might put up, I knew where his real sympathies lay. At any rate, I could but try him. So I went home and sounded him.

My father compressed his lips and looked at me shrewdly. 'An uncle and a nephew, you say, Dick? The uncle a sailor, I understand, recently home from a voyage. Nobody I know, I presume?'

'I'm sure you have never set eyes on him, sir,' I said. 'I haven't seen him myself yet.'

'Humph!' said my father. 'And the nephew, Dick – what about him?'

'I believe, sir, he will be – some sort of an honest farm hand.'

'Humph!' said my father again. 'I wasn't aware that the Jewels had any relatives on the land. But they appear to be worthy people – by your account of them. And it stands to reason they would wish to do what is only natural on this – very sad occasion. Yes, I think I may say I will make the application for them; but it must be understood that they are unknown to me personally. So that' (my father gave the smallest of chuckles) 'in the remote chance of any question arising later, I can truthfully assert that I know neither their appearance nor their whereabouts.'

The application was sent. The permission was granted; and armed with this precious document, Harry and I set out one early morning on our long ride: I in homespun coat and breeches borrowed from one of Trembath's gardeners, and with my hair cut a bit ragged, and my face deeply tanned; Harry in sailor's trousers, short coat and coloured neckerchief, with gold earrings, curled grey whiskers, silvered hair, rounded shoulders and lined face, all complete. Lady Trembath had made him up so cleverly that I wouldn't have known him myself; and every now and then I had to bid him speak, to make sure I wasn't riding with a stranger.

We were well entertained along the way; for everywhere we found the folk loud with indignation at the prisoners' fate, and the women, especially, full of tearful sympathy for their sorrowing relatives. All this heartened me greatly, for I knew that on our return journey we should have to look to these same folk for our protection and shelter.

Digory Whear, and another stout fellow in Trembath's employ – a man called Malachi Pascoe – had set out by a slightly different route with two fine horses. These horses, should any question arise, were a present from Lady Trembath to her 'dear cousin Rosalba Howard' of Dunhevet. But whether or no this cousinship was genuine, I really can't say.

I must explain that because of the riots in the city Matthy and Job had been removed from Exeter prison, and were now in Dunhevet jail, which made our journey the shorter, and the task of rescue easier, Dunhevet being but a small town and just within the borders of our own county.

We timed our visit to the jail for after dark, an easy matter in the winter, and quite in accord with our characters as two journey-worn travellers who had come from such a distance to take their sorrowing leave of relatives, had spent all their little stock of money on the way, and had now nothing left for a night's lodging. But the true reason for an after-dark visit was to screen Digory and Malachi, with whom we had foregathered that afternoon on the moor outside the town, and who were now waiting in a court at the back of the jail with the spare horses.

The turnkey who let us in to the prison was a small, thin man. I did not doubt that he could be easily overpowered, without too much damage to himself, when the moment arrived. I was carrying under my coat a length of rope with which to bind him, and in my pocket a sufficiency of wadding and a kerchief to gag him with. We had agreed that I was to be spokesman, while Harry should be too overcome with grief to utter a word – and well enough he acted; though indeed I never met a Cornishman yet who couldn't act. For myself, putting on my best Cornish accent, I handed the turnkey our pass, and asked 'ef it wud plaise un to bring we to a sight of his prisoners, for to bid they two poor vellans our sorrowing farewells'.

'It's a bad business,' says he, shaking his head. 'And I'm in mortal sorrow for they two myself.' Which made me immediately think that it might not be necessary to knock him down and bind him, after all.

By way of conversation, I became voluble about our tedious journey, the bad roads, and 'poor old Uncle Jacob's rheumatesum', while Harry shook his head, and clutched his knee and groaned. Then, thinking it best to know what we were up against, I asked the turnkey if it was usual to leave him all alone in charge of two desperate men.

He said he had a mate, and they took turns, guarding and sleeping; but that his mate had been called away that afternoon 'for to bring in a rogue of a poacher'. But as for the prisoners, they were secure enough, being in irons.

'Well, let's get to a sight of en for a foo mennuts, ef you plaise,' said I. 'For us hev a long traipse to go home, and I'm thenkin' a foo mennuts be most all Uncle Jacob be fit fur. 'Tes a shock for the poor old saul; he's all down-danted as you kin see, but he wouldn't rest till come.'

The turnkey then took a candle and we followed him down a stone passage and into a tiny cell, where Job and Matthy sat on a bench, each chained by the ankles to a staple in the floor. Two haggard wretches they looked, with sprouting beards and a thick growth of whisker; but they started up with exclamations of delight when we came in.

'Why, Dick! Why, Dick!' they cried, and then turned to gape at Harry.

''Tes your poor old Uncle Jacob,' says I, 'as hev traipsed all 'cross county for to see 'ee. Spake to 'en, uncle.'

'Well, boys,' began Harry with a gulp. But, at his first words, a great gurgle of laughter rose up in Job's and Matthy's throats. 'Uncle Jacob! Uncle Jacob!' they cried, grasping him by either arm and thumping him heartily on the back. 'Ef this bain't the best surprise of all our lives, for we thought never to see thee no more!'

The little turnkey set the candlestick on the floor. 'I'll give you boys one hour,' said he, 'and that's the most I can do for 'ee.' And with that he ambled out, locking the cell door behind him.

One hour! We didn't need that long! In one minute

we had told Job and Matthy our plan for their escape, and in another minute we had set about filing off their irons, keeping up a loud conversation the while, and Harry making the stone walls ring with his lamentations to cover the rasping of the file. When the irons were off, the two prisoners began to prance about the cell like mad things, so that I had to warn them not to make so much noise, even while the old joyous daring look that came back into their eyes made me feel like singing. We handed them each a pistol; and when, at the end of an hour, the key once more turned in the lock and the jailer came in, he found four pistols pointed at him simultaneously.

'Stand!' says Job, very low.

'Stand!' says Matthy.

'Not one step more!' says I.

'Or you're a dead man,' says Harry.

He was so taken aback that for a moment he could not utter a word. His face looked small and shrunk and deadly pale in the candlelight. He swallowed several times, and then at last found his voice – a very small, shaken, husky voice.

'Four to one,' says he. ''Tes murder, that's what 'tes.'

'No such thing,' says Harry. ''Tis you to raise no clamour but let us pass, and sharp, too; and your life's as safe from we as if you was in your mother's arms.'

The poor man fluttered his hands and moaned. 'I've always wished you boys well,' said he, 'and you know it. But 'tes as much as my life is worth to let 'ee pass. 'Twill be a hanging business, I shouldn't wonder, aiding and abetting. And if my mate was here, you wouldn't dare!'

'Oh yes, we would,' says Job, 'dare twenty of 'ee. Stand back from that door now, or you'll get a bullet in your brains. In a hurry, we be. Can't stay for argument.'

I had already uncoiled the rope from about my waist;

and, at sight of it, a gleam of relief came into the poor man's eyes.

'Well, if you take and bind me up, I can't help meself, I s'pose,' he said. 'Though I could lie and holler, all the same.'

'I've a gag handy,' says I, as we trussed him up, unresisting.

'Arra then, put it in my mouth,' says he, 'for how am I to stop 'ee? But don't throttle me, boys, for you know I've a kind heart.'

'Wishing 'ee no ill,' says Harry, as we dumped him, bound and gagged, on the bench. 'But no time to stop. Leave us half an hour to get on our way, and you'm welcome to wriggle yourself free of them lashings – they ain't that tight – and raise the town, if you've a mind to.'

The poor wretch rolled his eyes upon us and nodded. We left him the candle for company, and ran out round the corner into the court, where Digory and Malachi waited with the horses. In a moment we were all mounted and away, galloping up the street. Doors opened, windows flew up, there were shouts and running feet, but the gleam of our pistols kept folk at a distance. Fast, fast, and faster we went through the streets and down the hill out of the town, hearing behind us the confused clamour of many voices, and now the frantic and discordant ringing of the church bells. We turned in our saddles then, and fired our pistols into the air, and so uphill again, and on to the great moor that stretched for many miles westward ahead of us.

All through the night we galloped, and arrived at dawn at a solitary farmhouse, where we demanded, and were willingly granted, shelter. That day we lay snug in the farmer's hay-loft; and the horses, unsaddled, were driven a little way over the moor to graze among a herd of moor ponies. The town guard was out in search of us, so we heard, but their search must have been half-hearted. I know they must very much have preferred not to come up with us; for was not the smuggler a 'public benefactor', and was it not to everyone's interest that he should remain unmolested in his peaceful calling? The farmer, with many a chuckle, told us that they had passed by his place, looking neither to right nor to left, and had not so much as glanced at our grazing horses, though one of these same horses had actually crossed from one side of the track to the other in front of their very noses – from the farmer's description I concluded it was Diamond. And long before we came down from the hay-loft the town guard were cheerfully trotting on their way back to Dunhevet, having thankfully given up the search as a bad job.

So we proceeded on our way, lying up by day, riding by night, making detours to avoid the few small towns that lay on our route, but boldly using the turnpike road when it served us, and being let through the gates by willing hands. On the third night we arrived at Lord Trembath's, and were greeted by his lady with tears in her eyes and the merriest of smiles on her lips, and found Zach half crazy with joy to see his brothers.

But the whole exploit seemed to me to have been absurdly easy; and I could almost have wished there had been greater danger in it – if only that I might have proved myself more heroic in the eyes of Zach.

21
Up before the Mayor

It was in the small hours of a November night that we were at last able to smuggle the now fully recovered Zach, and his three brothers, safely out of St Mewes and aboard a fishing-smack that would carry them to Roscoff. There was no danger that night of interference by Hawkhurst, whom the friendly connivance of Boslowe and Carnquay fishermen had lured away to patrol the north coast. This was Lady Trembath's idea – she was a joyous intriguer – and I had taken a ride over to the north coast to arrange it. For several nights, now, these fishermen had been flashing signal lights, and bringing their donkeys to the beaches, and behaving altogether in a suspicious manner. It was a game they entered into with glee – and how was Hawkhurst to know that it was a put-up job? We had him nicely fooled and out of the way. As for the land-riders – Tidecombe and his gang – we had to risk falling foul of *them*; but for Tidecombe himself we had little respect (we were prepared to give him a crack over the head, if necessary), and we knew his men to be mostly sympathetic. Anyway, it was a risk that had to be run.

The previous night Zach and his brothers had lain hidden with some friends of Lady Trembath's in a manor house on the outskirts of St Mewes; and at two in the morning I went with them down to St Mewes Bay, where a boat was waiting to row them out to the fishing-smack.

It was just eighteen months now since that night when

I had hidden myself among the crab pots in the stern of the *Mayfly*, in my foolish attempt to accompany Zach on his venture to Roscoff. Now he was off to Roscoff again; and I, now as then, was to stay behind. Yes, it was only eighteen months, but it was to me like half a lifetime, as if in the interval I had grown from a silly lad into a man.

But, lad or man, as I stood in the darkness on the beach, and listened to the stealthy sounds of the oars as the boat drew away from me, there never was a heart more torn between grief and joy than mine was then: joy that Zach was at last safe, grief at my parting with him; for who could tell at what dim time in the future – if ever – I should see him again? I flung myself down on the sand with my arm over my eyes; I felt as lonely and desolate as if I had been washed up on a desert island, with everything that was familiar and dear to me snatched for ever out of my life.

'See you soon again, boy Dick,' Zach had said, as he grasped my hand at parting.

'See you soon again, soon again, soon again' – the words ran through my mind in a mocking refrain. For it was 'never, never, *never* again' that seemed to me more likely.

I don't know how long I had lain there, when a small sound – the slur of a footfall on the sand, and the intake of a breath – made me aware that I was not alone. I leaped to my feet with an angry cry. 'Who's there?' I exclaimed sharply.

' 'Tis only me, Dick,' answered a voice out of the darkness. 'Only old Roger.'

Kappen! The last person in the world I wished to meet at that moment! Zach gone, Kappen still with me: this indeed was added mockery!

'Go away!' I cried. 'What are you doing here?'

'Same as yourself, by what I can make of it,' said Kappen. 'Sorrowing for the loss of our poor boys.'

'What do you mean?' I demanded. 'They're nothing to you!'

'Oh, ain't they?' answered Kappen. 'Oh, ain't they?' He laughed softly. 'Haven't I told 'ee, Dick, as your friends is dear to me?'

Something in his laugh, something in the smug way he spoke, grated on me so acutely that I could have struck him I turned and ran from him up the beach ... And ran straight into the arms of two Excise men, who leaped up from nowhere, it seemed to me, grappled with me, overpowered me, and led me away between them to the Town Hall.

In the Town Hall I found Tidecombe and one of his riders, together with the mayor of St Mewes, a fat little man, who looked pale and puffy and worried and dishevelled, without his wig, and with his coat hanging askew from his shoulders, as if he had been waked from his warm bed in a hurry, and summoned most unwillingly to his official duties. He kept glancing from Tidecombe to me, blinking his sleepy eyes, and repeating, 'I know nothing about it, gentlemen. I assure you, I know nothing.'

Neither did I know anything, however much they pestered me ... What was I doing in St Mewes? Visiting friends, to be sure! ... What friends? Well, was it likely I would tell them when they took that suspicious way with me? ... On the beach? Certainly I was on the beach. Couldn't I take a walk on the beach at any time I felt like it? It was a free country, wasn't it? ... I worked myself up into a rage, which was easy in the mood I was in then, and threatened Tidecombe that he would hear from my father – yes, and from Lord Trembath, and many more such influential people, about this unlawful assault upon my person . . .

Smugglers? *What* smugglers? What had I to do with smugglers? That, I concluded, was Tidecombe's business, and Captain Hawkhurst's – it was certainly none of mine . . . Did I know that Captain Hawkhurst was away patrolling the north coast, and that it was now suspected he had been lured there? Well, really! What a question! Captain Hawkhurst didn't honour *me* with his confidence! . . . Did I know anything about a fishing-smack hovering out in the bay an hour or so ago? If I was on the beach, hadn't I seen her? No, I had *not* seen her. (That was true, for she was showing no light) . . . But I must at least have seen a rowing-boat? And what if I had? Why should I take notice of one rowing-boat more than another?

At this point the mayor seemed to rouse himself. He cleared his throat, pulled his coat into place, did up the buttons, and spoke decisively.

'Gentlemen,' said he, 'as you know, a boat with some of my men aboard has already been dispatched in pursuit of that smack, so why worry a poor lad who evidently knows nothing of any suspicious business. His father is a respected friend of mine, and I wouldn't say but what you may be heading for trouble in that quarter. As the lad himself has pointed out, this assault on his person is questionable. And, in short, wouldn't it be wiser, under the circumstances, just to let him go?'

He turned to me. 'Now, Richard Pellew, look me straight in the eyes, and tell me this. Do you solemnly swear that to your knowledge no acquaintances of yours have this night set out on a venture across the water?'

'A venture, sir?' says I vaguely.

'Yes, yes, you know what I mean by a venture. The

illicit bringing over of prescribed goods, without, in short, even paying duty on 'em.'

I looked him straight in the eyes, and, 'I solemnly swear it,' says I. I kept a straight face, but I could have laughed aloud. For I knew without a doubt now that the mayor was on Zach's side, and that the boat which he had sent in pursuit (about which I had felt a moment's panic) would not go very far, and would return without any news of the fugitives.

'Pardon me,' began Tidecombe, 'but it's not a question of contraband, it's a question of –'

'Pardon *me*,' interrupted the mayor. 'If it's not a question of contraband, why did you drag me from my bed, and what are we all doing here at this time of night?'

'It's a question of –' began Tidecombe again, and again the mayor interrupted him.

'At any rate, whatever it's a question of, I don't think we need detain this young fellow any longer. Get along back to your friends, Richard – they must be worried about you.'

'Good night sir,' I said, holding out my hand. 'And thank you.'

'Good night, my lad,' said he. 'No need to thank me.'

He shook me by the hand, and – yes, he actually winked at me! I bowed coldly to Tidecombe and his mate, and walked out with my nose in the air. The excitement of this little interview had somewhat overlaid my grief at parting with Zach; but that grief came back upon me in full force as I went to fetch Diamond from the shed where I had left him, and took my solitary way over the long miles to home.

Nor were my spirits cheered when I joined my father at dinner that day. After the briefest of greetings, he spoke no further word to me, good or bad, till the meal was nearly over; but his distended nostrils and drawn-down mouth warned me that he was in no amiable mood. I guessed that he must have got knowledge of my adventure at the Town Hall, but how he had got knowledge of it so quickly I could not imagine. I was puzzling my head about this, when he suddenly spoke.

'Dick,' said he, opening and shutting one of his thin hands that rested on the table, 'I give you freedom to come and go at your own sweet will. I impose no restraint on you. I ask no questions. And in return – what do I get? Nothing but trouble. If you can't keep yourself out of mischief, you'll kindly oblige me by seeing to it that your mischief does not involve your father. If trouble should come upon me at any time through any act of yours, I warn you I shall turn you to doors, sir. Yes, that's what I shall do, turn you to doors. And you may go and join any rascally associates you may have formed, on any foreign beach you fancy, for all I care!'

I tried to explain that such trouble as he might have in mind was not of my seeking. But he wouldn't hear a word. He wiped his lips on his napkin, got up from the table, said he did not wish to know what I was referring to, and left the room.

Was ever anything so unjust? Even if it *was* only a passing irritation on my father's part, it was most unfair! I sat there and moped, feeling that I hadn't a friend left in the world. Until I was roused by a quiet opening of the door, and there was Neil standing at my side, with his round eyes fixed on me like some faithful dog's, and his copy-book in his hand.

Oh well, I might as well devote my time to him as to anything else! But to be 'patient and tender' with him, as Parson Lanyon had exhorted me to be, was beyond my power that day; and I'm afraid I lost my temper and spoke angrily, more than once. And then the sad look that came into the poor fellow's eyes at my hot words only increased my irritability, knowing myself to blame, and not wishing to admit it.

22

Black Madge's Chair

That night there was a wreck. A vessel came in on the rocks, to the east of Garrick Sands, under the precipitous Garrick Head, and not a soul was saved from her. It was a shock to us all; for though there was a high sea running, the wind was offshore, and what she was doing so near the rocks was a mystery none could explain. Nobody had seen her come in, nobody had heard her strike; and it was not till early next morning that a labourer, down looking for driftwood in a gully among the cliffs, had seen her broken hull, and come rushing to the parsonage, shouting the news.

After that, it seemed no time at all before we were all

on Garrick Head, with the roar of the waves in our ears, looking down into a sun-glittering commotion of great breakers that washed and eddied and fell away from a long, black jag of half-submerged rock, across which the vessel lay broken in two – heaving with every uprush of the oncoming waves, and sinking back as the waves hurried over her, to spend their fury in spouts of foam against the cliffs.

The only sign of life about the vessel was a shag that stood perched on one of the rolling masts; and when he dived into a wave and disappeared there was no life down there at all: only the vessel, forlorn and broken in its heaving wretchedness.

But later that day, when the tide ebbed, a broken boat was found jammed between two rocks in a small cove nearby, as if those on board had launched her in a last desperate effort to save themselves.

Next day the bodies began to come in, and men risked their lives scrambling down the cliffs to bring them up, that they might have Christian burial in the churchyard. And, as Parson Lanyon remarked, if those bodies were singularly bare of any small possessions, and even of boots and coats, who were we to blame poor folk for helping themselves to what was of no further use to the dead?

'We bring nothing into the world, and we take nothing out,' said Parson Lanyon. 'And least said is soonest mended.'

But there was another, and more unusual, fact about those bodies. They had wounds on them that could not be accounted for by the battering of the sea. The conclusion we came to was that the crew must all have been drunk, and in the fighting out of their private quarrels, had lost all sense of where they were, and the danger they were in, until too late.

But not long afterwards, on a wicked black night, we were startled by seeing flares shooting up into the darkness beyond these selfsame cliffs. Roused by the flares, we were all out along the cliffs at midnight: to look down, with the wind whipping about our ears, into howling blackness, to hear cries of distress rising faintly out of the roar of the waters – to hear those cries and to be powerless to help; and, with the coming of day, to find the same tragic happening of a goodly vessel smashed, and no one left to tell how it had chanced.

And then there came a third wreck in the same place; and by this time the whole countryside was buzzing with the wildest rumours. What should bring these ships driving in upon our cliffs in this incomprehensible manner? Of this last wreck (it was the *Gannet* of Swansea, bound for Priddymouth with a cargo of coal) there were some survivors. For the night, though very dark, was not tempestuous. The crew had managed to launch two boats, one to be swamped immediately, the other to be driven in on Garrick Sands, and though there she had been capsized by the buffeting of the breakers, eleven men from her had managed to reach shore.

They were a sorry sight in the grey of early morning, as they came staring and staggering into the Pure Drop Inn, their water-dripping clothes hanging about them in shreds, and blood and seaweed dark about their lips. And, when dried and warmed and comforted with brandy, they had a strange tale to tell. For they swore they had seen the riding-lights of other vessels in the darkness ahead of them; and, thinking they had arrived at the opening of Priddymouth Estuary, they had steered straight in, making for safe anchorage. They spoke, too, of a monstrous black Shape, that stood among the breakers and thrust them away from land with huge arms and hands brandishing an axe; and of how, with the merciful coming of day, it had vanished, or they would none of them have escaped to tell the tale.

Riding-lights? *What* riding-lights? How could there be riding-lights in the sea under our treacherous cliffs, which never a vessel could approach without danger? And what was this monstrous Shape? The men must be out of their senses!

But the crews of three vessels could hardly be out of their senses, and it began to be whispered that the devil must be abroad; or, if not the devil himself, then that familiar spirit of his, a creature that went by the name of Black Madge. Everyone knew about Black Madge, though no one, in our day, had seen her. It was said that she sat in a niche on the top of Garrick Head (Black Madge's Chair, it was called), weaving spells to rouse tempests, and screaming to the doomed seamen to come to her withered arms. And, though none alive had seen her, many a one had heard those screams, like a mad laughter in the night, when the wind was high.

'If *she* be up to her tricks again,' said one man to another, 'then God help us all!'

Being intensely puzzled, I asked Parson Lanyon if it were possible that such a creature really existed.

'No, my boy, no,' he said. And then, after a long pause, 'At least I consider it highly improbable. We must seek for other explanations, Dick, before we let our minds dwell on this one. Though, surrounded from birth by mysteries, as we are, and knowing of the workings of the universe precisely nothing – who are we to say what is and what is not possible?'

I left him, feeling as puzzled and dissatisfied as when I had sought him. And, then and there, I came to a daring resolution. I would prove it for myself, one way or the other. I would keep watch on the cliffs at night; and though I felt that if I did see such a creature I might die of terror, I should at least *know*. And in my arrogance (or folly, if you will) I was not content, as Parson Lanyon seemed to be, to know 'precisely nothing'.

So, the next night, buttoned up in my greatcoat, with some food in one pocket and a pistol in the other, I set out to keep my eerie vigil. I had something else, too, in my pocket, and that was a handful of the silver *reals* which my mother and I had gathered out of the sands on that far-away night of the wreck of the *Gracia a Dios*. I had hesitated quite a time, scoffing at myself for my superstition, before I had made up my mind to open that treasure box of mine and take out these *reals*. But *if*, amid 'the working of the universe', to use Parson Lanyon's expression, there was room for such existencies as Black Madge, then surely it was wise to arm oneself with the only known defence against them – silver bullets?

The night fell very dark around me as I made my way towards the cliffs. There had been a slip of a waning moon to cheer me on starting out, but she soon went down the sky to westward and disappeared beyond Jewel's Cove, and the darkness closed in the more gloomily after her, with a scud of clouds and only a star or two blinking here and there between them.

As I neared Garrick Head the roar of the sea came louder to my ears, and the piled-up shapes of the huge cliffs rose in dim outline in front of me: shapes of towers and pillars, and the flat heads of dragons, and couched lions, and seated giants. I was familiar with them all, with their particular contours and their individual names – they were old friends in the sociability of daylight; but now, heaped together in the darkness, they became unfamiliar and menacing. There, on the top of the highest cliff, but hidden from me at this point by intervening pinnacles, was the straight-sided niche of rock that went by the name of Black Madge's Chair, and, descending from it on the sea side, were the irregular lumps of flattened boulders that were known as her ladder.

On a slant of sward to the landward of the Head I stopped and peered about me apprehensively. Exactly what I was looking for, I could not have said, but it seemed that my eyes would rather look anywhere than up at the Head above me. For suppose when I raised them my eyes should behold some monstrous and unnatural Shape perched on its rocky chair – what then? Who was I that I should presume to pit myself against the power of such appalling presences, if such existed? And, if they did not exist – what was I doing here in the darkness, with my pistol and my silver ammunition?

To my excited senses the booming of the sea seemed to be full of voices. What were they saying? I listened: at first to a jumble of unintelligible sounds, which presently seemed to sort themselves out into words:

'The hour is come!' they roared. 'The hour is come! The hour is – COME!' The reverberation of some huge hidden wave as it hit the cliff brought that word thundering to my ears. And then another voice made answer in a muttered undertone:

'Yes, the hour – the hour – but not the man!'

I turned and fled down the greensward with the hair rising on my scalp.

I did not pause to look back and up to see whether anything sat in that chair or not. I had seen nothing, but I had heard enough: my one idea was to reach home and the safety of my bed, and I must have run and stumbled some hundred yards or so before shame brought me up.

'Dick Pellew,' I said to myself, *'you are an arrant coward!'*

And I remembered Zach's words to me, 'If you find yourself afeared of aught, boy, *draw nigh to un*. For if you take and run from it, it'll be after 'ee, and stick in your mind like any plague.'

Well then, I *would* draw nigh to it! I would be true to Zach's counsel, for when had Zach's counsel ever failed me? I remembered those three wrecks, also, and thought on the drowned men; and it seemed to me that if I did not get to the bottom of the mystery, I should be failing in some self-appointed duty to the dead – and to the living who might yet have to die. I walked back determinedly, stood where I had stood before, and raised my eyes to the top of the cliff.

Nothing. The lumpy shapes of the rocks black against a rift of starlit sky, with the steep niche in the midst of them; but no awful Shape sat in that niche, no light swung there in darkness, no huge withered arm raised itself to beckon the doomed over the water: only the immobile rocks, the glitter of a star or two, and the booming of the waves that had no words to speak to me any more. Well, what had I expected? I laughed in my relief.

And then, suddenly, my mouth went dry. There *was* a light, and it was coming towards me, rising and falling with the slow, swinging motion of a light at a ship's masthead, moving along the cliffs – or in the air, for all I knew – but surely and steadily approaching the place where I stood.

No, I would not run, I would *not* run: be it devil or ghost I would 'draw nigh to it' – not a second time should I have to brand my name with cowardice! I took my pistol from my pocket, charged it with one of my silver *reals*, and so, armed against whatever supernatural enemy was coming my way, but with my heart, I must confess, jumping like a frightened rabbit against my ribs, I crouched down and began to move stealthily forward towards that unseen Thing with the light, which was equally stealthily approaching me.

The light seemed to be moving close to the ground, and it was coming along a flat edge of cliff to the eastward of Garrick Head. As it rose and fell, I could see a glint cast here and there upon the surface of the rocks, and I could see, too, a revolving of many shadows round it. Shadows of limbs, they seemed; not of two arms or two legs, but of many, as of a progression of several terrible things clustered together. Or, worse still, of one Thing, crawling on many legs. My courage all but failed me. I did not turn and run; I would face it, whatever it was; but I could not move a step farther. I crouched where I was, on the flat edge of the cliff, and waited.

Nearer and nearer, and ever nearer drew that swaying light with its revolving shadows, until it was so close that I could see what it was. And if, in one sense, my horror of it decreased, in another sense it grew greater. It was no ghost, it was no devil, unless, indeed, a devil in human shape: it was a man leading a horse, a big man in black wearing a black mask, and a big black horse. The horse had a lantern tied to its neck, and its head hobbled down to a foreleg, so that, as it moved, the lantern rose and fell, rose and fell, with the motion of a ship's light at sea. I knew the horse; and, mask or no, I knew the man.

'You!' I leaped upon him with a shout of rage; and, in the instant, Kappen's great hands were around my throat: my breath rattled, lightning danced inside my head, and then came a vast emptiness, into which, it seemed, I tumbled headlong.

23
In the Clutch of a Killer

'Clever, weren't you, Dick – or so you thought. But not clever enough. Nay, not clever enough by half. Come now, open them eyes of yourn, you ain't dead yet. You and me has to have a little talk, afore you go round land. But go round land you must, Dick, all in good time. A pity, too; but it seems 'tis either you or me, and no man is willing to go afore he's forced to. Now why did you want for to go and meddle, Dick? I told you I was your friend, didn't I? And I *was* your friend, being grateful for what you done – see? But you took agin me, Dick; yes, you took agin me, and that hurt me, it did. And then when it comes to spying on a man's private concerns – well –'

The voice, with a kind of wheedling malice in it, talked on and on. I thought I was having a bad dream, and struggled to wake. I opened my eyes, and there was Kappen's ugly yellow face close above me. I tried to lift my arm to blot out the nightmare of that face; but I could not lift it. I shut my eyes again, and there was the voice, still talking.

'Now don't go for to pretend you'm in a dead faint, because you ain't. I was forced to give you a bit of a squidge, but that weren't nothing; so open them eyes agin quick, and give heed to me.'

With that there fell a deluge of water over my face and neck, and I came to my senses.

It was no nightmare. Kappen *was* there, bending over me; and I was lying on the floor of his cottage, and my arms were tied to my sides with ropes, and my feet were bound together likewise. My throat ached, and my head spun, and I felt sick and weak.

'How – dare you?' I muttered. But the words sounded feeble and silly in my own ears; and so dazed I was that I don't know that I was greatly surprised, or even greatly annoyed, to hear Kappen laughing.

'Come,' said he, 'we must do better'n that, Dick, for you'm going to give me a fair hearing. I wouldn't go for to deny you that, nor yet myself, seeing as how what's come about was none of my choosing. So take a drink of this here bottle, Dick, and cheer yourself up a bit, and then us can talk it out, all fair and proper.'

He forced brandy between my lips, and I gulped it down; and it came upon me, at last, that I was in dire straits, and that I must keep my wits about me, and watch and listen, if ever I was to save myself.

'I'll take a drop meself,' Kappen was saying, putting the bottle to his own lips, 'for to hearten me for what I have to do. And, mind you, Dick, there never was a man sorrier about all this than old Ralph. Yes, 'tis Ralph, not Roger. But what a man's called is sometimes best kept quiet; and when you come out so sharp with "What's your name?" that day on Garrick Sands, I had to think quick – see? And that's how Roger Kappen come into this world, as you might say. Howsomever, Ralph they christened me, and Ralph Curnow I be – no need to keep that from you now. You can take that secret with you where you're going. And should you meet with any in that place as is curious about me, I permission you to tell 'em all you know. I can't say no fairer than that.'

He gave a horrible chuckle at his ghoulish joke.

'By the looks on your face, you've heard tell of Ralph Curnow?'

I had heard of him. There was a time, some years back, when the whole of our county was ringing with the evil deeds of this same Ralph Curnow: a pirate and wrecker who haunted our north coast, and who had earned for himself the title of Bloody Ralph by his murderous deeds. It was said that in return for his soul, the devil brought him wrecks in plenty; and it was said, too, that no seaman escaped alive from those wrecks. For, should they escape the waves, Bloody Ralph would knock them over the head with his axe, or cut off their hands as they clung to the rocks. An added horror about this man was that no one had ever seen his face, for he always went masked; and it was even rumoured that he was himself no mortal man, but a fiend in human shape. And then came the day of his capture, and men breathed freely again.

'But – but Ralph Curnow was hanged,' I stammered. 'I know he was!'

'So it seemed,' said Kappen. 'But that was an unfortunate mistake. 'Twas another poor fellow. I witnessed agin him myself. I didn't like to do it, but was force put; for 'twas better he hung than me.'

'You – devil!'

'Now don't you go for to use no rough words, Dick,' said Kappen reprovingly. 'You should know better nor that. A man's life is all he got. Look at it fair and square, now. If t'were some other body laying on the floor tied up instead of you, and you to go free, you'd feel sorry for him, oh yes, certainly, but you'd be gladder than you'd be sorry – because it wasn't you.'

I turned my head from him, and answered nothing. My loathing of the man rose up and choked me.

'So then,' he went on, 'I joined up with that there crew of pirates, but they was too squeamish for me, and so we fell out, and how they treated me you know. Aye,' says he, leaping up, 'but I'll get even with them yet! Even with 'em, ha! ha! And more'n even!'

He began to stamp about the room, waving his long arms, shouting and laughing. 'He's mad!' I thought, and turned faint with the horror of it.

'How will I do it, asks you? I'll do it this here way. I'll wreck every vessel what sails these waters till *they* come along, as come they will, you may be sure, one night sooner or later. Aye, they'll come in slap on them there jaggedy rocks, boy, what'll crack the timbers from under 'em like so many egg-shells; and there'll be old Ralph a-looking on and laughing. And should any try to save hisself there'll be a hatchet all ready for to jowd 'em up with – head or hands it makes no difference to Ralph. I've done as much afore, and I can do it agin.'

He came over to my side, stooped, stared at me with his glittering eyes, and dropped his voice again to its tone of wheedling malice.

'That there Dutchy of yourn – that Neil – what lost his voice – and a lucky chance t'was for him as he did lose it, or old Ralph would 'a been forced to lose it for him – *he* could tell 'ee. But he dursn't, Dick, no he dursn't. He knows too well what would happen to him.'

'And I know well what will happen to *you*!' I cried, with a sob of sheer terror and self-pity. 'Oh, maybe I shan't live to see it, but you'll swing, and your filthy carcass will hang in chains where all the world can see it, and the crows will pick out your horrible eyes!'

'Harsh words, harsh words,' said Kappen. 'But I forgive 'ee freely. Me heart is all soft towards 'ee, Dick, knowing what's afore 'ee. But Roger Kappen won't swing, and old Ralph' – he laughed – 'well, he's swung already, ain't he? Nay, all Roger Kappen's sins, for his little bits of smuggling aboard that there pirate ship, is now forgove him. Do you know what I've a-got in me pocket? I've a-got the King's pardon, I have. How did I get it? I got it for keeping me eyes open. And who did I get it from? I got it from Cap'n Hawkhurst, to be sure, along of the news I carried him 'bout your friend, Zach, and the comings and goings of the *Little Peter*.'

'Then it was you – it was *you*!'

'I'm proud to say it was, Dick. For 'twas a tidy piece of work – secret, as you might say, and with some risks to it, had your friends found me out. Aye, old Ralph had to be rare and sly over it. Told you Hawkhurst was biding his time, didn't I? But 'twas me what was doing that. Had to keep in with Parson, I had. And them tinners, too –

couldn't risk their getting wind of me doings. And then, when it seemed all was plain sailing, you got away to Trembath's. Well now, never mind for that. 'Tis all plain sailing for Roger Kappen now; he's a useful member of the public, he is. And not a poor one, neither. See here!'

The wretch walked over to a cupboard in the wall, and took out a leather bag. 'Just you hark!' said he, coming back at a run to chink the bag against my ear. 'Hear them merry little boys at their games inside? Do you know where they come from? They come from the King's Treasury!'

Devil! Traitor! Madman! Oh, if I had but known! Oh, if I had only relied more on my instinctive mistrust of the man, and watched him more closely! The *Little Peter* gone, Zach a fugitive, myself, it seemed, to lose my life, and all because we had welcomed this devil into our midst! I cursed the fatuous Christianity of Parson Lanyon, I cursed my own dullness, tears of rage flowed down my cheeks and into my mouth. I writhed on the ground, struggling against the ropes that bound me: if I could but get one hand free, and strike one blow into that ugly leering face, I felt I could almost be content to die.

'I'll hear no more!' I cried.

'I don't know as there's any more for 'ee to hear,' said Kappen. ''Cept that this here money bag might 'a been fuller, if you hadn't fooled Hawkhurst in the end. You did me out of three hundred pund over that job, Dick, and I take that as unfriendly of 'ee, I do. I had me suspicions about it, too; but a man can't be everywhere to one'st. And I couldn't follow 'ee when you rode off to the north coast, and keep me eyes open for Jewels to the south, all at one and the same time. Maybe, too, the north coast ain't so healthy a spot for me, neither, though the other fellow *did* swing. But I warned Hawkhurst, I did, as he was likely being fooled, and if he'd heeded me, we'd have nabbed them boys, Zach and the rest, come to the end. And if Tidecombe had been smarter, and you and that there mayor less sly, we'd have nabbed 'em, Hawkhurst or no. Some might bear 'ee a grudge, Dick, for that trick of yourn on the north coast, but old Roger can't find it in his heart to blame 'ee. For I like you, Dick. And 'cause I like you, I owed it to us both to 'splain things. And I've 'splained 'em ... So now, as the night won't last for ever, us best get going.'

'Going?'

'Well now, you didn't go for to suppose I would leave you hereabouts?' said Kappen. 'I'm tidy in me ways, and folk lying about is apt to tell tales, even' – he sniggered – 'when their mouth be shut.'

He stooped and lifted me off the floor, his great arms taking my weight as easily as if I had been a bundle of straw. Then, of a sudden, he laid me down again.

'Dick,' says he, 'you'm a pretty lad, and I ain't forgot you once did me a good turn. Me heart warms towards 'ee, spite of all. But you see, Dick, I can't let 'ee go for to spoil my little game, and tell tales on me and my lantern, or I won't get even with them as I've pledged me mind to get even with. But I'll trust you, Dick, in one thing. Folk like you is different from a man like me. I know you to be of that kind as keeps their promises. So now, pledge me your word as you'll keep all dark concerning Roger Kappen, and I'll cut them ropes from about you, and you can walk out here free's a bird, and us'll be friends from this day forth.'

I shut my lips tightly together, and made no answer.

'Come,' says Kappen, 'think on it, Dick. 'Tis warm and bright down home, a-setting by the fire; but 'tis cold and dark in Trevy Pool. No man ever found the bottom of it yet, so I'm told, save them as find it with a stone fast to their feet. And there don't come no spring, nor no summer-time down there. Just you give a thought to that, Dick. Aye, I can tell by the way you'm a-shivering and a-shaking, as you *be* giving thought to it. And what harm will it do 'ee, just to hold your tongue?'

'No, no, no!' I babbled out. 'If I must die, I must die! But I'll make no bargains with you, you dirty swine, and all I can say is, may the fiends torment you in hell for ever, for ever!'

'Well then,' said Kappen with a sigh, 'us must get going.'

While I struggled and flung myself from side to side, and tried to roll myself along the floor away from him, nay, and more than once set my teeth in his hairy hands, he made a noose round my chest with a piece of rope, and taking the two ends of rope in his hands, swung me up on to his back, blew out the lamp, and strode off into the night.

To struggle now was worse than useless, for it did but draw the noose tight about my ribs and cause me agonizing pain. And, after one or two moments of such pain, I gave up, and hung limp. Meanwhile Kappen's voice went sounding through my ears in a husky undertone.

'You best keep quiet as a little mouse, now, Dick. For I warned 'ee, should you think to give a shout, 'twill be the last thought as ever you'll have. But you be still free to change your mind. You won't? Well now, that's a pity, that is. But you shan't suffer, Dick, I promise 'ee; for though you took agin me, I never took agin you. There'll be a crack on the head for 'ee, sharp and sudden, afore you go under. Feel this fist?' He took the two ends of the rope in his left hand, and tapped his right fist against the top of my head. 'He was known as Ralph's hammer, once 'pon a time – a hammer what never gave no second blows.'

All this time he was walking steadily forward up the hill on to Trevy Downs. It came to my mind, and my heart beat wildly at the thought, that the way to the pool lay not far from the tinners' hut. If I were to save my breath now, and give one wild shout for help when we neared the hut, it might be that the tinners would hear and come to my rescue. A forlorn hope! For had I not been warned what would happen if I shouted? Yes, a forlorn hope; but my only one, and so I clung to it. I began to reason wildly. I clung to desperate tag-ends of hope. Some tinner might even still be abroad, help might be nearer than I thought. I mustn't give up! I must keep alert, on the watch for any small chance of rescue.

All my senses now seemed to become preternaturally alert. Pressed against Kappen's back as I was, and in the dark, you would suppose that I could see nothing; but it seemed to me that I could see the very grease marks on his shoulders, and the smell of his jacket came sickeningly strong to my nostrils. And every sound – the movement of his feet over the grasses, the breath in his body, the low swish of some branch as a small wind shook it, the straining and tiny creaking of the ropes he held me by – came to my ears like pistol shots, so clear, so loud, that I seemed never to have heard anything in my life until that time. And when a rabbit leaped from the undergrowth and scuttled away to the side of me, I could have screamed out for the sharp pain of its loud going. But I heard no movement of human help, no stir of footfalls except Kappen's, no friendly human breath: we were alone, the murderer and I, and all around us in the dark stretched the desolation of Trevy Downs, and ahead of us – that pool!

No, listen! We were *not* alone! Something breathed in

the night, close to my side, a quick, sighing breath, so low that at any other time I should never have heard it. And it is certain that Kappen did not hear it, for he was talking again in that husky undertone. But what he said I did not hear. Quiet fingers were cautiously – oh, so cautiously – feeling their way down my bound right arm, and there came a rasping of the cord at my elbow. The cord parted, my arm was free, a knife was slipped into my hand. Then the sighing breath died away behind me, and it was only Kappen talking in his husky undertone.

'Dick, you bain't fainted away, be 'ee? I'm being so kind as a man can be, and if I was sure you was fainted away, I'd give 'ee a touch of Ralph's hammer now, so I would, so's you wouldn't come round no more. But if you *bain't* fainted away, I wouldn't go for to do no such thing; for you know, Dick, as I told 'ee, life is all we got, and I reckon no one would want to cut it short, even by five minutes. And maybe, come to the end, you'll pledge me your word, same as I asked, and live to see dawning day.'

My heart was thumping so loud that I felt surely he must have heard it. I couldn't bring myself to answer him, but I feigned to struggle, that he might know I was conscious. I doubled up my knees and kicked with my bound feet against his back. I flung myself from side to side till the tightening of the noose about my ribs caused me such pain that I found myself groaning. And all this time I was working away with the knife to sever the cord that bound my feet. The cord parted and fell to the ground; I held my feet together and struggled and groaned to cover the sound of its falling, which seemed to my excited senses like the boom of a cannon.

'There, there,' Kappen was saying, 'don't you go for to hurt yourself the like of that. I wouldn't have 'ee hurt,

Dick. Say a little word in my ear 'bout that there promise, and you and me'll agree yet. But it ain't no manner of use you fidgeting like you be, for I've got 'ee tight.'

I put my lips up to his ear. 'Murderer!' I whispered. 'Fiend! Devil! Those are the only words you'll get from me!'

'And I'm sorry to hear –' Kappen began. But in that moment I had cut through the noose about my ribs, thrust the knife with all my force into his neck, and slid from his back.

'Help! Help! Help!' I shouted at the top of my bursting lungs, and fled away into the darkness.

I heard Kappen give a roar of pain. I heard his feet floundering after me. I heard a shot behind me, and one long, unearthly scream; then many feet running, and a voice I did not know, calling 'Dick! Dick!'

I ran towards the voice ... And stumbled into the arms of Neil.

24
Neil's Story

'Aye,' said Tom Treva, 'you owe him your life, boy, that's sartin sure. He followed you up to Kappen's place, and hearkened like a fox with his ear agin the door to all that was said. And when he knew how things was planning out, he come up here faster nor the wind. And was we surprised when we hear him talking, him as we thought dumbfoundered! I should say we was! But there waren't much time to be surprised in. We took us guns, and out we come, and he took the knife – 'twas his own notion that, and a smart one, for us dursn't shoot the devil, you see, with you a-hanging on his back. So us waited nigh the pool, and Neil he ran, and came up behind you, and put that knife in your hand. And when us heard you shout, why then 'twas time for we to act.'

'And – Kappen?' I asked.

'Well, you heard un squeal, didn't 'ee?' said Tom. 'Don't you think no more 'pon him. He's gone where he thought to put you; and had us known the games he was playing, he'd have gone there long ago... And that's the only pity of the whole issue,' he added, puffing thoughtfully at his pipe, 'that he didn't go there long ago.'

I was sitting in the tinners' hut, by their blazing hearth, with their rough, friendly presences crowded round me. I felt somewhat lightheaded, and every now and then a shudder ran through me. But these shudders, violent at first, were becoming every moment less and less. For I was safe! The fear of death was gone. The terror of the last few hours was falling away from me, as the terror of a nightmare falls away – though still remembered – with the blessed opening of the eyes.

I think, though, that I cannot have been quite in my normal senses, for the fact that Neil had found voice and spoken did not strike me then as extraordinary. I just didn't think about it. I sat there in a kind of doze, looking into the flames, and hearing the friendly voices about me less and less distinctly, until I fell into a dreamless sleep.

When I woke, some time in the afternoon of the next day, the tinners, of course, were away to their work, and there was no one in the hut but Neil and myself: I, stretched before the fire, with a rough blanket to cover me, and a bundle of fern under my head, Neil busy throwing fresh faggots on the blaze.

'Are you rested?' I heard him saying.

Then indeed I sat up in astonishment, flung the blanket from me, and stared at him incredulously. 'Neil!' I exclaimed, 'you can speak!'

'Yes, I can speak, Dick.'

'Tell me how – tell me why –' I stammered.

'I am not frightened any more,' said Neil.

'Frightened?'

'Of *him*. Of –' But even now, it seemed, he could not speak Kappen's name. 'Though I *was* still frightened,' he went on, 'when I listened at his door, and when I ran up here. But I was frightened for you then, more than for myself. And I *had* to speak to save you, so my throat was loosened, and words came. Though it didn't seem like me speaking; it seemed like – someone else.'

'And does it still seem like someone else?'

'Oh no,' said Neil, 'because *he's* – gone.'

'Tell me about it,' I said.

'Eat first?' said Neil.

I found I was ravenously hungry, and the stew that was simmering in a crock over the fire smelled deliciously. Neil brought a tin dish and ladled me out a goodly helping, and I ate it gratefully, washing it down with draughts of the best ale I seemed ever to have tasted. And all this while Neil was silent, so that it almost seemed that I had dreamed he had found his voice, and that now he would never speak again. At last, when I could eat no more, I put the dish down at the side of the hearth and said:

'Neil, if you can really speak, if it isn't just a wild dream, and if I am in my senses, for the love of heaven – what does it all mean?'

He told me his story then, simply and rather flatly, looking into my face all the while with never a smile or a frown.

He was born, he said, in a small village in Holland, and had early lost both his parents. An uncle, who kept a little saddler's shop in Rotterdam, had sent him to sea as a ship's boy in a small trader, and it was when they were passing up the north coast of Cornwall, being bound for Cardiff, that they were wrecked in a gale one early morning off the slate rocks of Penvose Head.

'*He* came – that man came,' said Neil, 'when we were struggling in the water. The captain was clinging to a rock. *He* swung his hatchet, and the captain was gone, and there were only his hands with the fingers grasping the rocks, and the blood running from the wrists. I was close by, washed up on to a ledge, with the waves flowing over me, and the ship's cook was there beside me on the same ledge. *He* took me up by the neck with one great hand, and the mask slipped from his face, and I saw it. He was about to dash my brains out against the rocks, when the cook grabbed him by the legs, and he let me go and went for the cook with the hatchet and cleft his skull through. And so he served them all – all but myself, who dived down under the water – for you know I can swim well, Dick – and came up on the far side of a rock and got ashore and hid. And though I heard him looking for me, he didn't find me.'

He had lain hid all through that day, he told me, and when it was night he had got up and run, not knowing where he was going, running in sheer panic, till at dawn he came to a house in a valley under a church that stood on a rise, and there he fell at the door of the house and was found by a lean man, whom he took to be a priest, and was brought into the house, and lay there, he did not know for how long, in a delirium. And when he came to himself he found he could not speak. A vision of Kappen's cruel face and that bloodstained hatchet seemed to fill his whole mind and his whole world, and it was as if Kappen's hand were still at his throat, stifling back any word he tried to utter. But in his pocket was a bit of a card with his uncle's address in Rotterdam, and though the letters were soaked and blurred with the salt water, the priest managed to make them out, and got him sent back to Rotterdam on a tea-trader.

'But when I came to my uncle's shop,' said Neil, 'I found him gone, and a stranger there in his place; so I ran about the town looking for him, but still I couldn't speak, and all the time I was seeing that – man with the hatchet, and his hand was at my throat. So I came at last down on to the docks, and was there picked up by the captain of a schooner in need of a boy, and the rest you know. But you cannot know – for no one ever can, how that – man haunted me. I thought if only I could get the sight of him out of my mind, I might find my voice again. And then suddenly, there he was, not a vision but the man himself, and I seemed to be living in a frightful dream from which I could never more wake. And I knew you despised me for my cowardice, and because I liked you, and would have you think well of me, that was almost worse than all.'

I have set this down in plain English, because I cannot attempt to give the true savour of Neil's speech, with its slightly thick, but quite pleasant, Dutch accent. His last words made me feel ashamed. For it was true, I *had* despised him – and now I owed him my life.

'God forgive me, Neil!' I said. 'And you forgive me, too, if you can. For without you, where should I be at this moment?' I thought of the bottomless depths of Trevy Pool, and shivered. 'Neil, take my hand, and say you forgive me. And if my whole life can do it, I will make amends.'

'Oh,' said he, and the tears came up and glittered in his eyes. 'I have never had one friend in the world, till I met with you.'

'Well,' I said uncomfortably, 'I expect we best say no more about it, and I think it's time we both went home.'

'Home!' said Neil, a little sadly.

'Yes, home,' I answered. 'My home and yours, for ever and a day. You know, Neil, I never thought of it before, but it will be splendid to have a brother.'

With that he gave me a broad smile, and we set off back to the manor, I having left a note for the tinners to thank them, printing my words large and clear, and hoping that one of them might be able to read it.

I had a problem in front of me, and that was what I should say to my father. It seemed to me he must be told; if only to account for Kappen's disappearance, and Neil's miraculous finding of his voice, and the strong determination I had formed that Neil should no longer be a servant in the house, but my companion and adopted brother. But how to tell my father all this, I couldn't think. Knowing the twists of his peculiar mind, I realized that he would not welcome a plain tale from me, with its mention of circumstances of which he chose to feign ignorance. I decided I would tell my tale, then, first to Parson Lanyon, and leave it to him to explain to my father as best he could. So, instead of going straight home, I went with Neil to the parsonage. And there, having told the parson that I had strange news for him, I poured out the whole story.

Except for an occasional 'God help us!' or a 'Tut, tut, tut!' Parson Lanyon listened in silence, turning his eyes from one to the other of us with a most comical expression of dismay and astonishment. When I had finished he leaped up from his chair, grasped Neil's hand and shook it heartily, and then did the same by me, exclaiming brokenly that he was a silly old man, and that the ways of the wicked were completely beyond him. Then, after pacing the room once or twice, he came to stand before me, looking very solemn, and abstractedly twiddling one of the buttons of his coat.

'Dick,' said he, 'I own I made a most grievous, a most calamitous mistake. But I cannot help feeling, in spite of everything, that I erred in the right direction. As a humble servitor of that Being who, we are told, "hateth nothing that He hath made", and "sendeth rain on the just and on the unjust", I cannot help feeling that I see most clearly when I see only the good, and leave the rest to Heaven. And so I beseech you, Dick, and you, too, Neil, my lad, to put aside all memory of evil. Forgive, and also forget. For,' says the parson, twiddling his button so hard that he twiddled it right off his coat, 'there can be no forgiveness while the memory of the wrong is still held in the mind ... There now,' says he, 'I've been preaching at you, and I've lost my button. Oh, thank you, Dick.' (I picked the button up from the floor for him, and he thrust it into his pocket.) 'Yes, yes, of course, I will go straight away and tell your father. Leave it to me.'

What he said to my father, I don't know, but it was, at any rate, something very satisfactory. For my father sent a message to me through Nathaniel that Neil was to take his supper with us; and when we went into the parlour he greeted us both with a most surprising cordiality.

'So, Dick,' says he, 'I hear that you have taken to yourself a brother. And in that case, without troubling ourselves to inquire too closely into the circumstances, I conclude that I am now blessed with a second son. Come, take your place here by me, Neil, my boy – don't stand on ceremony ... And as for you, Dick,' he went on, raising his eyebrows and giving me a quizzical smile, 'on the whole, you're a good enough lad; and if at times I speak querulously to you, that, you must understand, is a father's privilege.'

We spent the happiest of evenings after that. I had never known my father in a pleasanter mood.

25
Home Again

I was happy in my new companionship with Neil, to whom, as the months passed, I became more and more attached. I found him a thoroughly good fellow; perhaps, compared to us Cornish, a bit stolid in his wits, and a stickler for what he deemed right, arriving at conclusions slowly, and, having once arrived at them, refusing to budge from them upon any consideration whatsoever. So that I still caught myself being impatient with him at times. But, apart from the great fact that I owed him my life, I liked him heartily; and I dare say – for I am vain at bottom – my liking was not lessened by his attitude to me, which was one of open admiration. It seemed I was his hero, just as Zach was mine – though I am sure Zach was never flattered by *my* adulation, whereas I was by Neil's.

Parson Lanyon applied himself with great energy to Neil's education, and that did not make me lazier, you may be sure. For it did not please me that Neil should get ahead of me in any way. And this was a good thing, and kept my mind occupied, so that I could not be so continually fretting over Zach's absence. Though I *did* fret; I thought about him very often, trying to picture where he was, and what he was doing. And to have no news of him gave me that desolate feeling of being washed up on a desert island.

I frequently went up to Jewel's Place, to pester Zeb and Sarah; but they knew nothing, and could tell me nothing. My visits reduced Sarah to wailing tears over the fate of her 'poor handsome boys', and Zeb to goblin-like wrath, and the most blood-curdling curses on 'that Hawkhurst'. Strangely enough, it was in old Gracie Winkey that I found most consolation.

'Don't 'ee fretty, my lover,' she said to me. 'They'm coming back all in good time. Aye, coming back frolicsome as the birds in May.'

And when I asked her how she could be so sure of that, she looked at me with a kind of mocking twinkle in her sea-dark eyes, and said she had 'tidings'.

'Tidings?' I asked eagerly. 'Have you heard? Has someone seen them and brought news?'

'Hark to 'un!' said she, with a high cackle of laughter. 'Who should have seen 'em, if not old Gracie? I've seen 'em walking on these cliffs, aye, many's the time. And I've seen 'em down to Cove of a night-time, a-launching of the *Mayfly*.'

'Oh, but,' I cried, 'that's only fancy!'

'You can call it fancy in the ignorance of your mind,' said Gracie grandly. 'But I see things what other folk don't see. And what I see do come to pass.'

I think, because I wanted so much to believe her, I did believe her, and it strangely comforted me.

Even without the Jewels, Hawkhurst had a busy winter of it. What with the troubled state of the times, and the high taxes, smuggling was everywhere on the increase. For us, in our far-away corner of the country, it was still a kind of game of hide-and-seek between Hawkhurst and the rest of us: a game played in the dark by small groups all round our rocky coast, with the Revenue cutter distractedly and ineffectually sailing from one trouble spot to another, and Tidecombe, as distractedly and even more ineffectually, galloping his riders from one end of the county to the other. None of us came to grief. The only 'tongue-tabbas' that perhaps the county had ever known had gone where his tongue was silenced under the waters of Trevy Pool.

But very different tales came drifting down from up-country: tales of smugglers in armed bands, seven hundred strong, riding together to guard their wagons of contraband goods from the coast to London; tales of bloody battles between masked free-traders and unwilling troops, of desperate fights at sea, of murders, of hangings. Tales over which we shook our heads, demanding to be told why people couldn't let each other alone.

But it seemed that people couldn't let each other alone. England couldn't let America alone: we were at war, and though at first that seemed a little thing, as the months passed, and the years passed, it became a big thing; and fewer and fewer men could be spared for patrol work. Certainly none could be spared to patrol our remote shores. Hawkhurst was called away, and went to fight his country's battles on a man-of-war; Tidecombe was called away, together with all his men, to struggle with the desperate bands of free-traders on Romney Marsh, and to get shot in the back for his pains, poor fellow. We were left entirely to our own devices, and the smuggling game, as many were heard to complain, lost much of its savour, there was now so little danger in it.

Things went from bad to worse: France signed a treaty with America, Spain entered the war against us, Britain's command of the sea was lost, and her state desperate. Taxes and the price of living soared, and the up-country smugglers had it their own way, with little of authority left to oppose them. It was said that 'a foreign visitor to England, travelling the Dover road to London, might have imagined he was back in fourth-century Italy, as he encountered the armed hordes riding unhindered with their booty from the coast to the capital'. And, while Parliament framed law after law, only to have those laws flagrantly broken, the voice of authority was heard to exclaim, 'Will Washington take America, or the Smugglers take England first?' The bet would be a fair and even one.

And what of Zach? What of Zach in all this turmoil? Over and over again I asked myself that question. Was he still eating out his heart in idleness across the water? Had the French shut him up in jail as an enemy? Or had he perhaps been pressed into the navy, and forced to take up unwilling arms against his fellow men? Was I never to see him again? Yes, I *would* see him again, if he were still above ground. I promised myself that when this war was over – and I didn't seem to care much how it ended – I would take ship and go in search of him, first to Brittany, and, if I didn't find him there, then round the world, if need be.

Such thoughts were continually in my mind. And then, one summer dusk, just about the time when the last lark had dropped to the ground, and the blackbirds were sounding their good-night chatter, I was moodily pacing the moor behind Jewel's Place, when I saw the house door open, and a man step out. He went round by the front of the wall, and stood there, gazing down over the sea.

For a moment I thought that, like Gracie Winkey, I was seeing things that other folk did not see. Then I gave a great shout:

'Zach! Zach!'

Yes, there he stood, with his black curly hair, and his sunburned smiling face, and the scar across his nose – Zach in the very flesh!

'Why, Dick,' said he, coming to meet me, 'I scarce did know you, you've grown to be a man!'

'You've come home, Zach, you've come home!'

'Yes, Dick boy, we've all come home. For France wouldn't keep us, and America won't have us, and Hawkhurst be gone, so what was to stop us? I was on my ways down to have a look at the old *Mayfly*. Zeb have kept her shipshape, he tells me, so she'll be on the water tomorrow, or next day, I shouldn't wonder ... Nay, not for a week or two, though, come to think of it, for there's a thing more important to do first.'

'And what's that, Zach?'

'Just for me and Janey to get wed,' said Zach. 'And if

you're not too proud,' he added almost shyly, 'I'd ask 'ee for to be my best man.'

Too proud! What could he be thinking of? Pride pointed exactly the other way.

'I'm bursting with pride that you should ask me, Zach,' I said.

And with all my heart I meant it.